学做中国菜
Learn to Cook Chinese Dishes
禽蛋类　Poultry ＆ Eggs

外 文 出 版 社
FOREIGN LANGUAGES PRESS

前 言

朱熙钧

倘若不是想成为专业厨师，只是为了自家享用或偶尔待客而学做中国菜，大可不必专门去拜师学艺。中国主妇们的厨艺最初几乎都是从她们的老祖母和母亲那里耳濡目染学来的；待到为人妻母之后，她们当中的一些有心人，或借助菜谱潜心揣摩，或与友邻切磋交流，烹调出的菜馔有时竟然不逊于名店名厨的出品。当然，中国家庭中擅长烹饪的男士也比比皆是，况且饭店餐馆中的名厨以男性居多。

《学做中国菜》丛书的编撰者都是久在名店主厨的烹饪大师。为了使初学者易于入门，他们化繁为简，介绍了各类菜式的用料、刀法、制作步骤等；初学者只需按书中所列，一一去做，无须多日便可由熟生巧，举一反三，厨艺大进。

这套丛书共 9 册，分水产类、菜蔬类、肉菜类、米面类、汤菜类、冷菜类、豆品类、家宴类。本册为禽蛋类，共列有 40 种以禽肉、鲜蛋为原料的菜肴的制作方法。

禽蛋是烹制中国菜的重要原料，禽肉较畜肉细嫩、柔软、营养价值高且味道鲜美。蛋的营养价值更高，亦可烹制花色繁多的菜肴。本册介绍的禽蛋类菜肴所用的原料是人工饲养的鸡、鸭、鹅及其所产的蛋。

鸡的品种较多，一般分为肉用、蛋用、肉蛋兼用三种类型。烹制菜肴最好用肉用鸡。由于各式菜品的烹制方法不同，对鸡的大小、老嫩要求也不尽相同，如烹制"油泼鸡"、"香炸八块"、"清炖童仔鸡"等所需的是出壳几个月的雏鸡；而"宫保鸡丁"、"麻辣鸡丝"、"香酥鸡"等可用当年的鸡或剔肉或整只使用；隔年鸡营养丰富、味道鲜美，但肉质较老不宜炸或剔肉爆、炒，适用于整只或斩块酱、烧、炖。如"红烧鸡块"、"人参炖鸡块"等。

鸭有填鸭和麻鸭之分，填鸭体大、肉多肥嫩是烹制鸭菜的上品，可整只烹制如"烤鸭"、"姆油鸭"，也可斩成块烹制如"碧螺春炖鸭"，还可剔肉爆炒如"葱爆鸭丝"、"三鲜鸭条"等。麻鸭属肉蛋兼用鸭，肉质细嫩、味道鲜美，适于整只或斩块烹制，如"香酥鸭"、"清炖鸭块"等。

鹅的肉质较粗，可烹制的菜品较少。不过用整只鹅制成的"烧鹅"、"酱鹅"则是菜肴中的佳品。

鲜蛋是烹调的重要原料之一，可单一使用也可与其他原料合用。鸡蛋在烹制中用的最多，单一原料烹制的菜肴如："五香茶叶蛋"、"虎皮蛋"、"蛋松"等。也可作配菜如"蕃茄鸡蛋"、"蛋卷"、"蛋饺"等，还可作调料中挂糊、上浆用。鸭蛋是制松花蛋、咸蛋或糟蛋的最好原料。鹅蛋质地较老，较少用来烹制菜肴。

Foreword

Zhu Xijun

You don't have to take classes from a professional teacher to learn the art of Chinese cooking if all you want to do is to entertain your friends or cook for your family. Almost without exception, Chinese women learn this skill by watching and working together with their mothers or grandmothers. After they become wives or mothers themselves, the most diligent will try to improve their techniques by consulting cook books and exchanging experiences with their neighbors. In this way they eventually become as skilled as the best chefs in established restaurants. It should be noted, of course, that most of the well-known chefs in famous restaurants are men, because many men in Chinese homes are just as good at the art of cooking as their wives.

This book in the *Learn to Cook Chinese Dishes* series has been compiled by master chefs. They have used simple explanations to introduce the ingredients, the ways of cutting, and the cooking procedures for each Chinese recipe. Readers, who follow the directions, will before long become skilled in the art of Chinese cooking. The entire set consists of nine volumes, covering freshwater and seafood dishes, meat dishes, vegetable dishes, courses made from soy beans, soups, cold dishes, pastries, dishes of eggs and poultry, and recipes for family feasts. This volume introduces forty recipes of poultry meat and egg dishes.

Poultry is a major category of raw materials for Chinese cooking. Fowl meat is more tender and has a finer texture than animal meat. Besides, it contains more valuable nutrients and offers specially delicious tastes. Eggs have even better nutrients and can produce a wide selection of dishes. The meat and egg recipes used in the dishes presented in this book all use domesticated chickens, ducks and geese.

Chickens are raised for their meat, eggs or both. To cook chicken dishes, the ones raised for yielding meat are the best choice. Different dishes require chickens of different sizes and age. To cook "Sizzling Chicken", "Crispy Chicken" and "Stewed Tender Chicken", chicks several months old are used. To do "Stir-fried Chicken with Chili Sauce and Peanuts", "Spicy Shredded Chicken" and "Crispy Chicken", the meat from part of a chicken or a whole chicken of one year in age is called for. Chickens older than a year may be more nutritious and tasty, but the texture of its meat tends to be tougher and therefore not suitable for stir-frying. Usually such chickens are used either whole or in large pieces to be cooked or stewed with heavy seasonings. Examples include "Braised Chicken Chunks with Brown Sauce" and "Stewed Chicken with Gingko Fruit".

Ducks range from those that are force-fed and those that are naturally fed. The first category are larger in size and their meat is tender and fat, making them ideal meat for duck dishes. They can be cooked whole to make "Roast Duck" and "Stewed Duck in Earthen Pot", or cut into chunks to make "Braised Duck with Green Tea". Alternatively, chunks of meat can be taken from the duck to make "Quick-fried Shredded Duck with Scallions" and "Braised Duck Slices". The naturally fed ducks yield both meat and eggs. Their meat is fine in texture and tasty. Such ducks can be cooked in whole or cut into chunks to make dishes such as "Crispy Duck" and "Duck Stewed in Clear Soup".

Goose meat is comparatively tougher and rougher than chicken and duck meat and therefore can produce fewer dishes. But "Roast Goose" and "Goose with Bean Paste" made with a whole goose are choice dishes on any Chinese menu.

Eggs are a major ingredient in Chinese cooking either for making pure egg dishes or for combining with other ingredients. Chicken eggs are used most often and the pure chicken egg dishes include "Five-flavored Egg with Tea", "Egg with Brown Sauce" and "Fluffy Egg". Together with other ingredients, they can make dishes such as "Egg with Tomatoes", "Egg Rolls" and "Egg Dumplings". Eggs can also be used as a binder in other dishes. Duck eggs are employed to make "Hundred-year-old Eggs", preserved salty eggs and eggs preserved in rice wine sauce. Goose eggs are less often used in Chinese cooking because of their rough texture.

目　录
Contents

名词解释 Terms Used in Chinese Cooking

上浆： 猪肉丝、猪肉片、牛肉丝、牛肉片、羊肉丝、羊肉片、鸡肉片在烹制前都要上浆。上浆大多用于滑溜、滑炒、清炒、酱爆等烹调方法。上浆好坏，直接影响烹调出菜肴的质量。上浆就是把切好的肉，用水冲洗净，放入盐、料酒、淀粉(有时也放鸡蛋)，拌匀后，向一个方向搅拌，感到有劲为止。

Coating (*shangjiang*): Shreds and slices of pork, beef, mutton and chicken have to be coated before they are cooked in such ways as slippery-frying, quick-frying and stir-frying. And how the meat is coated has a direct bearing on the quality of the cooked dish. The coating process involves first washing the cut meat, then adding in salt, cooking wine, and cornstarch(sometimes eggs are also used) and stirring well in the same direction until you feel it is a bit sticky.

刀工 Cutting techniques:

直刀法： 就是指刀同砧板垂直的刀法，分切、剁、砍，切是一般用于无骨的主料，剁是将无骨的主料制成茸的一种刀法，砍通常用于加工带骨的或硬的主料。

Straight-cutting: Holding the knife perpendicularly over the chopping board to cut, chop and heavy-cut the main ingredient. Cutting is applied to boneless meat ingredients, chopping is done to turn boneless ingredients into pulp or paste and heavy-cutting is used when preparing meat with bones or other hard ingredients.

平刀法： 是刀面与砧板平行的一种刀法，分推刀、拉刀。推刀就是把刀从刀尖一直推到刀根，拉刀就是把刀从刀根拉到刀尖。平切就是把刀一切到底。

Horizontal-cutting: Holding the knife flat against the chopping board to push it or pull it through the ingredients.Pushing means to push the knife through the ingredients from the knife's tip through to its end while pulling involves going through the ingredients from the end to the tip of the knife.

斜刀法： 刀面同砧板面成小于 90 度夹角的刀法。

Slashing: To cut by holding the knife in an angle smaller than 90 degrees from the surface of the chopping board.

花刀： 是在主料表面用横、竖两种刀法的不同变化，切(不断)出花纹，经加热后，主料卷曲成各种形状的刀法，有菊花形花刀，麦穗刀，鳞毛形花刀等。

Mixed cutting: To cut straight and then cross with sideways cuts to produce varied patterns. When heated, the ingredients cut in this way will roll up into different forms such as chrysanthemums, wheat ears and scales, according to the ways they are cut.

片： 用切或片的方法将原料加工成薄片。质地硬的原料用切，质地软的用片的方法加工成薄片。

Slicing (*pian*): By either cutting or slicing to turn the ingredients into thin slices. Hard ingredients require cutting while soft ingredients require slicing.

丝： 丝有粗细之分，一般在 0.2-0.4 厘米左右。一般先将主料切成 0.2-0.4 厘米的薄片，再将这些薄片排成瓦楞状，排叠要整齐，左手按稳主料，不可滑动，用刀把主料切成丝。

1

Shredding (*si*): The thickness of shreds usually varies between 0.2 (0±08 in) and 0.4 cm (0±16 in). First, either chunks of meat or vegetables are cut into thin slices of 0.2 to 0.4 cm in thickness. The slices are then arranged neatly like roof tiles.Pressed steadily underneath the left hand of the chef, the slices are finally cut into shreds.

条：条的成形方法，是先把主料切成厚片，再将片切成条，条的粗细取决于片的厚薄。

Strapping (*tiao*):Main raw materials are cut into thick slices that are cut again into straps the size of which is decided by the thickness of the slices.

粒：粒比丁小些一般在0.3厘米见方，切的方法同丁相同。

Grain-sized dicing (*li*): Cut in the same way as diced pieces, they are simply much smaller in size. The most common size is 0.3 cm (0.12 in) each side.

丁：先将主料切成厚片，再将厚片切成条，然后再切成丁。丁有大小之分，大丁在2厘米见方，小丁在1厘米见方。

Dicing (*ding*): Main raw materials are cut into thick slices that are cut into straps. In turn, the straps are reduced to diced pieces that may be as large as 2 cm (0.8in) on each side or as small as 1 cm (0.39 in) on each side.

末：末比粒还小、将丁或粒剁碎就可以了。

Mincing (*mo*): Ground ingredients are even smaller than grain-sized dices.Usually the diced pieces are chopped into mince.

茸：用排剁的方法把主料剁得比末还细。

Chopping to make a pulp (*rong*): To chop the materials, knife cut after knife cut into pieces even finer than minced materials.

块：块是采用切、砍、剁等刀法加工而成的。块分菱形块、方块、长方块、滚刀块等。

Cutting into chunks (*kuai*): Chunks are the result of perpendicular and sideways cutting as well as chopping. The chunks come in many shapes such as diamonds, squares and rectangles.

炸：是旺火加热，以食油为传热介质烹调方法，特点是火旺用油量多。

Deep-frying (*zha*): Heat the cooking oil over a hot fire and deep-fry the materials. This process is characterized by a hot fire and a large amount of oil.

炒：炒是将加工成丁、丝、条、球等小型主料投入油锅中，在旺火上急速翻炒成熟的一种烹调方法。炒分滑炒、熟炒、干炒等几种。滑炒是经过粗加工的小型主料先经上浆，再用少量油在旺火上急速翻炒，最后以湿淀粉勾芡的方法，叫滑炒。熟炒是把经过初步加工后的半成品，改切成片或块，不上浆，用旺火烧锅热油，放入半成品翻炒，再加佐料而成。煸炒和干炒是把主料煸一下，在热油锅急火炒至退水后，加佐料，起锅。

Stir-frying (*chao*): Put processed materials in the shape of diced pieces, shreds, straps, or balls into the heated oil and quickly stir them over a hot fire. There are several different ways of stir-frying. *Hua chao* (stir-frying with batter), for example, requires that the ingredients are put in a batter and then quickly stirred in a small quantity of oil over a hot fire.The final process is to apply the mixture of cornstarch and water. *Shu chao* (stir-frying precooked food) does not require that the materials be put into some kind of batter. Simply put the precooked materials into the wok and use a hot fire before adding spicing agents. *Bian chao* and *gan chao* (raw stir-frying) calls for the simmering of main ingredients, then quick-stir-frying over a hot fire until the juice is fully absorbed. Now add spicing agents and the dish is ready to serve.

溜：溜是先将主料用炸的方法加热成熟，然后把调制好的卤汁浇淋于主料上，或将主料投入卤汁中搅拌的一种烹调方法。

Slippery-frying(*liu*): First deep-fry the main ingredient and then top it with sauce or mix the main ingredient in the sauce.

爆：爆是将脆性主料投入适量的油锅中，用旺火高油温快速加热的一种烹调方法。

Quick-fry over high heat (*bao*): Put crispy materials into the wok with medium amount of oil and quickly stir the materials over high heat.

隔水炖：隔水加热使主料成熟的方法，叫做隔水炖。

Steaming in a container (*ge shui dun*): Put the main ingredient into a bowl or similar container and cook it in a steamer.

烧：烧是经过炸、煎、煸炒或水煮的主料，再用葱姜炝锅后，倒入翻炒，然后加适量汤水和调味品，用旺火烧开，中小火烧透入味，改用旺火使卤汁稠浓的一种烹调方法。

Stewing over medium,then high heat (*shao*): After putting scallions and ginger into the wok, put in the main materials that have been deep-fried, or stir-fried or boiled and stirred. Then add water and seasoning materials to cook over a hot fire until the ingredients boil. Turn the fire to medium or low to allow full absorption of the sauce into the ingredients before turning the fire hot again to thicken the sauce.

扒：扒是将经过初步熟处理的主料整齐地排放在锅内，加汤汁和调味品，用旺火烧开，小火烧透入味，出锅前，原汁勾芡的一种烹调方法。

Stewing and adding thickening (*pa*): Neatly arrange the main ingredient that has already been cooked,add water and flavoring materials and cook over a hot fire until it boils. Turn the fire to low to allow full absorption of the flavor. Thicken the sauce with the mixture of water and cornstarch before bringing the dish out of the wok to serve.

煮：煮是将主料放入多量的汤汁或水中，先用旺火煮沸，再用中小火烧熟的一种烹调方法。

Boiling (*zhu*): Put main materials of the dish into the wok with an adequate amount of water and cook it over a hot fire to the boiling point. Then continue to cook after turning the fire to low or medium.

烩：将加工成片、丝、条、丁等料的多种主料放在一起，炝锅翻炒后，用旺火制成半汤半菜的菜肴，这种烹调方法就是烩。

Precooking and then stewing (*hui*): First heat the oil in the wok, put in scallions and ginger and then put several kinds of main ingredients that have been cut into slices, shreds, chunks or dices to cook over a hot fire so as to create a dish of half soup and half vegetables and meat.

煎：煎是以少量油布遍锅底、用小火将主料煎熟使两面呈黄色的烹调方法。

Sauteing (*jian*): Put a small amount of oil into the wok and use a low fire to cook the main ingredient until it is golden brown on both sides.

蒸：蒸是以蒸汽的热力使经过调味的主料成熟或酥烂入味的烹调方法。

Steaming (*zheng*): Cook the materials that have already been prepared with flavoring agents by using hot steam.

拔丝：拔丝又叫拉丝，是将经过油炸的小型主料，挂上能拔出丝来的糖浆的一种烹调方法。

Crisp frying with syrup (*ba si*): Put small-size ingredients that have already been deep-fried into sugar syrup heated in the wok. When diners pick up the materials, long sugar threads are created.

焯水：就是把经过初加工的主料，放在水锅中加热至沸(主要为去腥味或异味)，原料出水后供烹调菜肴之用。焯水分冷水锅和热水锅。冷水锅就是主料与冷水同时下锅，水沸取出，适用于腥气重血量多的主料如牛肉、羊肉等。热水锅就是先将锅中水加热至沸，再将主料下锅，翻滚后再取出主料。适用于腥气小，血污少的主料如鸡、鸭、猪肉和蔬菜。

Quick boiling (*chao*): Put main ingredients into the pot and heat the water to boiling point(in order to remove fishy or other undesirable smells). Then cook the boiled ingredients. The quick-boiling process includes cold water boiling and hot water boiling. The former requires putting the ingredients into the pot toge ther with the cold water and then taking them out when the water boils. This process is often applied to such materials as beef and mutton,which contain a fishy smell and a lot of blood. The latter calls for heating the water in the pot to boiling point before putting the ingredients in.This is applicable to materials like chicken, duck, pork and vegetables that have a much weaker fishy smell and less blood.

油温表

油温类型	俗　称	油温特点
温油锅	四成 70℃－100℃	无青烟，无响声，油面平静。
热油锅	五、六成热 110℃－170℃	微有青烟，油四周向内翻动。
旺油锅	七、八成热 180℃－220℃	有青烟，油面仍较平静，用勺搅动有响声。

Temperatures of cooking oil:

Category	Temperature	Features
Luke-warm	70ºC-100ºC 158ºF-212ºF	Smokeless, soundless, calm oil surface
Hot oil	110ºC-170ºC 230ºF-338ºF	Slight smoke, oil stirs from the side to the center of the wok
Very hot oil	180ºC-220ºC 356ºF-428ºF	Smokes, the surface remains calm and when stirred, sizzling sound is heard.

花椒：花椒是花椒树的果实，以籽小，壳厚紫色为好。味香麻，烹调肉类的调料。

Prickly ash (*hua jiao*): Seeds from prickly ash trees, which are small and light purple in color. They have a slight effect of numbness on the tongue. Used to cook dishes with meat.

椒盐：味香麻，是炸菜蘸食的调味品。把花椒和盐按 1:3 的比例在锅中，微火炒成焦黄，磨成细末，即成。

Pepper salt (*jiao yan*): This mixture is made by stirring one portion of peppercorns and three portions of salt in the wok until they turn crispy yellowish in color and release their fragrance. Then finely grind the mixture into powder. It serves as a seasoning for deep-fried dishes.

味精： 根据个人口味，也可不放味精，而使用适量的鸡精。

Monosodium glutamate and chicken bouillon: Though MSG is essential in traditional Chinese cooking, for many who do not find it agreeable, chicken bouillon can be used instead.

茴香： 小茴香是茴香菜的籽，呈灰色，似稻粒，有浓郁的香味。

Fennel seeds (*hui xiang*): Seeds of fennel plants, grey in color and similar to unhusked rice grains in shape, have a hot flavor.

大茴香： 又名八角、大料，形如星状，味甜浓，烹调肉类的调料。

Star anise (*da hui xiang*): In the shape of stars, they have a strong and sweet flavor. Mostly used in cooking meat dishes.

糟： 制作料酒剩下的酒糟经过加工就成为烹调用的糟，糟具有同料酒同样的调味作用。

Steaming with distillers'grains sauce (*zao*): Distillers'grains, which are left over from liquor making, are processed into a spicy agent for cooking that has the same function as the cooking wine.

五香料： 大料、茴香、桂皮、甘草、丁香(丁香花蕾)五种香料

混合为五香料，研成粉为五香粉。

Five Spices (*wu xiang liao*): A mixture of powdered star anise, fennel seed, cinnamon bark, licorice root and clove buds. Also referred to as the "five-powdered spices".

桂皮： 是桂树的皮，外皮粗糙呈现褐色。

Cinnamon (*gui pi*): The bark of cinnamon trees, brown in color.

料酒： 常用料酒是用糯米等粮食酿制成的，料酒，在烹调菜肴过程中起去腥、增香的作用，特别是烹制水产或肉类时少不了它。如没有料酒，可用适量的啤酒或白兰地代替，但没有料酒好。

Cooking wine (*liao jiu*): Cooking wine, brewed from grain, is applied to remove the fishy smell and increase the aroma of the dish. It is particularly essential when cooking dishes with aquatic ingredients and meat. While cooking wine is most desirable, in its absence, beer and brandy can be used.

勾芡： 勾芡就是在菜肴接近成熟时，将调好的湿淀粉加入锅内，搅拌均匀，使卤汁稠浓。增加卤汁对主料的附着力的一种方法。

Thickening with mixture of cornstarch and water (*gou qian*): When the dish is nearly cooked, put a previously prepared mixture of cornstarch and water into the dish and stir well so as to thicken the sauce or broth. This process promotes the flavored sauce to stay with the main materials of the dish.

勾芡作用： 1、增加菜肴汤汁的粘性和浓度。2、增加菜肴的光泽。

Major functions of this process: (1) Increase the stickiness and thickness of the sauce of the dish. (2) Making the dish look more shiny.

勾芡关键： 1、勾芡必须在菜肴即将成熟时候进行。2、勾芡时锅中汤汁不可太多或太少。3、必须在菜肴的口味、颜色已经调准后进行。4、勾芡时锅中油不宜太多。

Key for using this process: (1) This process must be conducted when the cooking of the dish is nearly complete. (2) The sauce in the wok must not be too much or too little when this thickening technique is applied. (3) This process can only be done after all efforts for flavoring and coloring of the dish are completed. (4) When doing the thickening process, the wok should not have too much oil in it.

如何使用筷子

　　吃中式饭菜一般使用筷子。筷子是用木或竹、骨及其它材料制成长25-30厘米、上方（各边为8毫米）下圆（直径为3-5毫米）的二根小棍。

　　使用时须依靠拇指及食指、中指和无名指的连贯配合。方法是：首先把两根筷子拿在右手，用食指、中指及无名指在距筷子近上端处各夹一根筷子，再把拇指和食指合在一起，如图1。用筷子取食时，把食指和中指夹的一根向上抬，另一根不动，使两根筷子张开。如图2。夹取食物时，把食指和中指夹的筷子往下压，夹住食物，抬起筷子进食，如图3。

How to Use Chopsticks

Chopsticks for eating Chinese food are usually made from wood, bamboo, animal bones or other materials. About 25 to 30

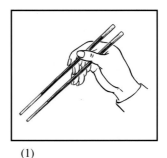

(1)

(2)

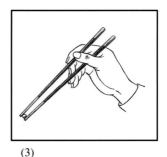

(3)

centimeters long, their top is square, about 0.8 square centimeter, and the low end round with a diameter of 3 to 5 millimeters.

The correct way of using the chopsticks requires concerted efforts of the thumb, index finger, middle finger and third finger. Hold the pair of chopsticks in the right hand, using the index finger, middle and third fingers to keep the chopsticks steady near their top and then push them open by moving the thumb and index finger. (See Drawing 1)

To pick things up with chopsticks, lift upward one of the two chopsticks with the index and middle fingers while keeping the other one where it is so as to separate the two. (See Drawing 2)

Once the chopsticks have picked up the food, press one of the chopsticks with the thumb and index finger and raise the pair. (See Drawing 3)

笼屉　蒸锅
Steaming tray(*long ti*)Usually made of bamboo or wood, these often come in several tiers

炒锅
Skillet

火锅
Hot-pot

砂锅
Earthen pot

汤勺　炒铲　漏勺
Soup spoon Shovel Perforated spoon

筷子
Chopsticks

菜（面）板
Chopping board

菠萝鸡片

主料：鸡脯肉 250 克

辅料：去皮新鲜菠萝 200 克

调料：油 500 克（实耗 75 克）、鸡蛋清 1 只、干淀粉 15 克、盐 3 克、味精 2 克、清汤 50 克、料酒 5 克

制作：①将鸡脯肉切成长 6 厘米、宽 2 厘米、厚 0.1 厘米的片，放入碗中加 20 克清水用筷子搅拌上劲，再放入鸡蛋清和盐 2 克、干淀粉 10 克搅拌上浆备用。菠萝去心，切成长 5 厘米、厚 0.2 厘米、宽 3 厘米的片，放入漏勺中。余下的淀粉用水化开备用。

②炒锅置旺火上烧热，倒入油，烧至四成热时，放入浆好的鸡片滑炒至断生，倒入放有菠萝片的漏勺中控净油。

③锅内留余油 25 克烧热，放入清汤、盐、味精、料酒，倒入湿淀粉勾成芡汁，再将鸡片和菠萝片倒入锅内迅速翻炒均匀，淋上少许麻油，装盘即成。

特点：鸡肉鲜嫩，菠萝香脆，色泽鲜明

口味：咸鲜适口

Chicken Slices with Pineapple

Ingredients：

250 grams (0.55 lb) chicken breast
200 grams (0.44 lb) fresh peeled pineapple
500 grams (1 cup) oil (only 75 g or 5 tbsp to be consumed)
1 egg white
15 grams (2 1/2 tbsp) dry cornstarch
3 grams (1/2 tsp) salt
2 grams (1/2 tsp) MSG
5 grams (1 tsp) cooking wine
50 grams (3 tbsp) water

Directions：

1. Cut the chicken breast into slices 6 cm (2.4 inches) long, 2 cm (0.8 inch) wide and 0.1 cm (0.04 inch) thick. Place in a bowl. Add 20 g (1 1/3 tbsp) of water and mix well with a pair of chopsticks until substance becomes sticky. Add the egg white, 2 g (1/3 tsp) of salt and 10 g (1 1/2 tbsp) of dry cornstarch. Remove the central part of the pineapple and cut the rest of the fruit into slices 5 cm (2 inches) long, 3 cm (1.2 inches) wide and 0.2 cm (0.08 inch) thick and place in a strainer. Soak the rest of the dry cornstarch in cold water.

2. Heat the wok. Add the oil and heat to 70-100℃ (160-210˚F) to slippery-fry the chicken slices for just about 1-2 minutes. Put into a strainer with the pineapple slices to drain off the oil.

3. Keep 25 g (1 2/3 tbsp) of oil in the wok. Add the water, salt, MSG, cooking wine, and the mixture of cornstarch and water. Now put in the chicken and pineapple and quickly turn several times. Sprinkle on a few drops of sesame oil and dish is ready to serve.

Features：The chicken is slippery and tender while the pineapple is crispy. Beautifully colored.
Taste：Fresh and salty to the taste.

菠萝鸡片
Chicken Slices with Pineapple

松仁鸡米

主料：鸡脯肉 250 克

辅料：松仁 100 克

调料：油 500 克（实耗 75 克）、鸡蛋清 1 只、味精 2 克、干淀粉 10 克、盐 4 克、清汤 50 克、干红辣椒 2 只、料酒 5 克、葱 10 克

制作：①将鸡脯肉切成 0.5 厘米见方的小粒放入碗内，加入蛋清、盐 2 克、淀粉 5 克搅拌上浆备用。松仁入油锅炒熟。干红辣椒及葱切 0.5 厘米长的段。

②炒锅置旺火上烧热，倒入油，烧至四成热时，放入鸡米滑炒至断生，倒入漏勺中，控净油。清汤、盐、味精、淀粉、料酒放入碗中调成芡汁。

③锅内留余油 25 克烧热，放入干红辣椒、葱段煸炒出香味，倒入调好的芡汁，再放入鸡米、松仁翻炒均匀，淋上少许麻油，装盘即成。

特点：色彩鲜艳，松仁香酥

口味：咸鲜适口

Chicken Cubes with Pine Nuts

Ingredients：

250 grams (0.55 lb) chicken breast
100 grams (0.22 lb) shelled pine nuts
500 grams (1.1 lb) oil (only 75 g or 5 tbsp to be consumed)
1 egg white
2 gram (1/2 tsp) MSG
10 grams (1 1/2 tbsp) dry cornstarch
4 grams (2/3 tsp) salt
50 grams (3 tbsp) water
2 dried red chilis
5 grams (1 tsp) cooking wine
10 grams (1/3 oz) scallions

Directions：

1. Cut the chicken breast into cubes 0.5 cm (0.2 inch) on each side. Place in a bowl. Add the egg white, 2 g (1/3 tsp) of salt and 5 g (1 tbsp) of dry cornstarch and mix well. Fry the pine nuts in a wok until they are done. Cut the red chilis and scallions into sections 0.5 cm (0.2 inch) long.

2. Heat the oil in a wok to 70-100°C (160-210°F) and slippery-fry the chicken cubes. Put in a strainer to drain off the oil. Put the water, salt, MSG, cornstarch and cooking wine in a bowl to make a sauce.

3. Put 25 g (1 2/3 tbsp) of oil in the wok and add the red chilis and scallions to stir-fry until they produce a strong aroma. Add the pre-made sauce, the chicken and pine nuts and turn several times. Sprinkle on some sesame oil and take out to serve.

Features：Beautifully colored with a strong fragrance from the crispy pine nuts.
Taste：Salty and delicious.

松仁鸡米
Chicken Cubes with Pine Nuts

宫保鸡丁

主料：鸡脯肉 250 克

辅料：花生米 150 克

调料：油 500 克（实耗 75 克）、鸡蛋清 1 只、干淀粉 12 克、盐 2 克、味精 1 克、酱油 10 克、糖 10 克、干红辣椒 2 只、葱、姜末各 2 克、清汤 50 克、料酒 5 克、麻油 5 克

制作：①将鸡脯肉拍松，刻上十字花刀，切成 1.5 厘米见方的丁，放入碗内，加入鸡蛋清、盐 2 克、干淀粉 10 克搅拌上浆。余下淀粉用水化开备用。花生米去皮后入油锅炒熟。干红辣椒切成长 1 厘米长的段。

②炒锅置旺火上烧热，放入油，烧至四成热时，放入浆好的鸡丁滑炒至断生，倒入漏勺中，控净油。

③锅内留油 25 克烧热，放入葱姜末、干红辣椒段煸炒出香味，放入清汤、料酒、酱油、糖、味精烧开后，用湿淀粉勾芡，倒入炒好的鸡丁及花生米，翻炒均匀，淋上麻油，装盘即成。

特点：色泽红亮

口味：香辣可口

Stir-fried Chicken with Chili Sauce and Peanuts

Ingredients：

250 grams (0.55 lb) chicken breast
150 grams (0.33 lb) peanuts
500 grams (1 cup) oil (only 75 g or 5 tbsp to be consumed)
1 egg white
12 g (1 2/3 tbsp) dry cornstarch
2 grams (1/3 tsp) salt
1 gram (1/4 tsp) MSG
10 grams (1 1/2 tsp) soy sauce
10 grams (2 tsp) sugar
2 dried red chilis
2 grams (1/15 oz) finely cut scallions
2 grams (1/15 oz) chopped ginger
50 grams (3 tbsp) water
5 grams (1 tsp) cooking wine
5 grams (1 tsp) sesame oil

Directions：

1. Beat the chicken breast with the side of a kitchen knife to soften the texture of the meat. Cut lightly to make cross-cuts on the meat. Then cut the chicken breast into cubes 1.5 cm (0.6 inch) wide each side. Place in a bowl. Add the egg white, 2 g (1/3 tsp) of salt and 10 g (1 tbsp) of dry cornstarch and mix well. Mix the rest of the dry cornstarch with water for later use. Fry the peanuts. Cut the red chilis into fine chips.

2. Heat the oil in a wok to 70-100℃ (160-210°F) and slippery-fry the chicken cubes for 1-2 minutes. Take out and drain off the oil in a strainer.

3. Put 25 g (1 2/3 tbsp) of oil in the wok and stir-fry the scallions, ginger and red chilis until they produce a strong aroma. Put in the water, cooking wine, soy sauce, sugar and MSG, and bring to boil. Thicken the sauce with the mixture of cornstarch and water. Put in the chicken and peanuts and turn several times. Sprinkle on sesame oil and dish is ready to serve.

Features：Shiny with brown color.
Taste：Spicy, fragrant and delicious.

宫保鸡丁
Stir-fried Chicken with Chili Sauce and Peanuts

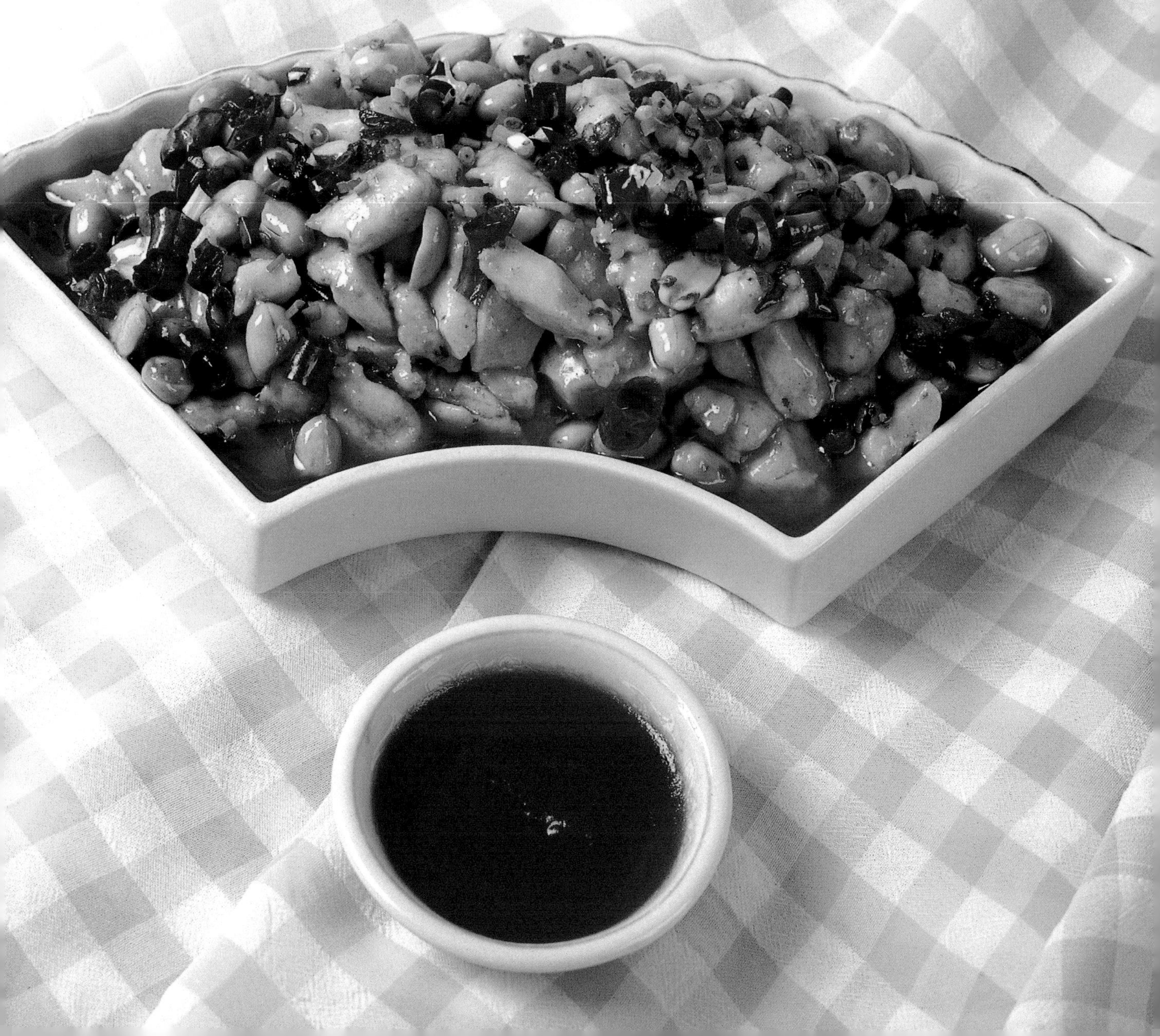

核桃鸡丁

主料：鸡脯肉 250 克

辅料：核桃仁 150 克

调料：油 500 克（实耗 75 克）、鸡蛋清 1 只、干淀粉 12 克、盐 4 克、味精 2 克、葱 5 克、姜 10 克、干红辣椒 5 克、清汤 75 克、料酒 5 克

制作：①将鸡脯肉拍松，刻上十字花刀，切成 1.5 厘米见方的丁放入碗中，加入蛋清、盐 2 克、干淀粉 10 克搅拌上浆。余下的淀粉用水化开备用。核桃仁入温水中浸泡，剥去衣，放入油中炸熟捞出。葱切 1 厘米长的段。姜切指甲片。干红辣椒切 1 厘米长的段。

②炒锅置旺火上烧热，倒入油，烧至四成热时，放入浆好的鸡丁滑炒至断生，倒入漏勺中，控净油。

③锅内留余油 25 克烧热，放入葱、姜、干红辣椒略煸炒后放入料酒、清汤、盐、味精烧开，用湿淀粉勾芡，倒入鸡丁、核桃仁，翻炒均匀，淋上少许麻油，装盘即成。

特点：桃仁香脆，鸡丁滑嫩

口味：咸鲜微辣

Deep-fried Chicken Dices with Walnuts

Ingredients：

250 grams (0.55 lb) chicken breast
150 grams (0.33 lb) shelled walnuts
500 grams (1 cup) oil (only 75 g or 5 tbsp to be consumed)
1 egg white
12 grams (1 2/3 tbsp) dry cornstarch
4 grams (2/3 tsp) salt
2 grams (1/2 tsp) MSG
5 grams (1/6 oz) scallions
10 grams (1/3 oz) ginger
5 grams (1/6 oz) dried red chilis
75 grams (5 tbsp) water
5 grams (1 tsp) cooking wine

Directions：

1. Beat the chicken breast with the side of a kitchen knife to soften the texture of the meat. Make light cross-cuts on the meat. Cut the meat into cubes 1.5 cm (0.6 inch) wide each side. Place in a bowl, add the egg white, 2 g (1/3 tsp) of salt and 10 g (1 1/2 tbsp) of dry cornstarch and mix well. Mix the remaining cornstarch with water. Soak the walnuts in lukewarm water, remove the fine skin and deep-fry. Drain off the oil. Cut the scallions into sections 1 cm (0.4 inch) long. Cut the ginger into small thin slices the size of finger nails. Reduce the red chilis into sections 1 cm (0.4 inch) long.

2. Heat the oil over strong fire to bring the temperature to 70-100℃ (160-210˚F) and slippery-fry the chicken cubes for 1-2 minutes. Take out and drain off the oil in a strainer.

3. Put 25 g (1 2/3 tbsp) of oil in the wok and stir-fry the scallions, ginger and red chilis until they produce a strong aroma. Add the cooking wine, water, salt and MSG and bring to a boil. Thicken with the mixture of cornstarch and water. Put in the chicken and walnuts and turn several times. Sprinkle on a few drops of sesame oil and take out to serve.

Features: The walnuts are fragrant and crispy while the chicken is slippery.

Taste: Salty and slightly spicy.

核桃鸡丁
Deep-fried Chicken Dices with Walnuts

青椒鸡丝

主料：鸡脯肉 250 克

辅料：青椒 150 克

调料：油 500 克（实耗 75 克）、鸡蛋清 1 只、干淀粉 12 克、盐 4 克、味精 1 克、料酒 5 克、清汤 75 克

制作：①将鸡脯肉切成 0.25 厘米见方、长 5 厘米的丝放入碗中，加盐 2 克、鸡蛋清、干淀粉 10 克搅拌上浆。青椒切丝。余下的淀粉用水化开备用。

②炒锅置旺火上烧热，倒入油，烧至四成热时，放入鸡丝滑炒至断生，倒入漏勺中，控净油。

③锅内留余油 25 克烧热，放入青椒丝煸炒几下，加清汤、盐 2 克、味精烧开后，用湿淀粉勾芡，放入鸡丝，翻炒均匀，淋上少许麻油，装盘即成。

特点：色彩悦目

口味：咸鲜适口

Shredded Chicken with Green Pepper

Ingredients：

250 grams (0.55 lb) chicken breast
150 grams (0.33 lb) green peppers
500 grams (1 cup) oil (only 75 g or 5 tbsp to be consumed)
1 egg white
12 grams (1 2/3 tbsp) dry cornstarch
4 grams (2/3 tsp) salt
1 gram (1/4 tsp) MSG
5 grams (1 tsp) cooking wine
75 grams (5 tbsp) water

Directions：

1. Cut the chicken breast into shreds 5 cm (2 inches) long and 0.25 cm (0.1 inch) thick and wide. Place in a bowl and add the egg white, 2 g (1/3 tsp) of salt and 10 g (1 1/2 tbsp) of dry cornstarch and mix well. Cut the green peppers into shreds similar to the size of the chicken shreds. Mix the remaining cornstarch with water.

2. Heat the oil in a wok over a strong fire to bring the temperature to 70-100°C (160-210°F) and slippery-fry the chicken for 1-2 minutes. Put in a strainer to drain off the oil.

3. Put 25 g (1 2/3 tbsp) of oil in the wok and stir-fry the green peppers by turning several times. Add the water, remaining salt and MSG and bring to a boil. Use the mixture of cornstarch and water to thicken the liquid. Put in the chicken shreds and evenly turn several times. Sprinkle on a few drops of sesame oil. Take out and serve.

Features：Invitingly colorful.
Taste：Salty and refreshing.

青椒鸡丝
Shredded Chicken with Green Pepper

麻辣鸡丝

主料：鸡脯肉 250 克

辅料：笋 150 克

调料：油 500 克（实耗 100 克）、鸡蛋清 1 只、盐 1.5 克、味精 1 克、清汤 75 克、干淀粉 12 克、料酒 10 克、糖 5 克、干红辣椒 2 只、花椒粉 1 克、酱油 20 克、葱姜各 5 克、麻油 5 克

制作：①将鸡脯肉切成 0.25 厘米见方、长 5 厘米的丝放入碗中，加入盐、鸡蛋清、干淀粉 10 克搅拌上浆。笋切成丝。葱、姜、干红辣椒切末。余下的淀粉用水化开备用。

②炒锅置旺火上烧热，倒入油，烧至四成热时，放入鸡丝迅速滑开，炒至断生，倒入漏勺中，控净油。

③锅内留余油 50 克烧热，放入葱、姜、干红辣椒末煸炒出香味后放入笋丝略炒，加入料酒、清汤、酱油、糖、味精烧开后用湿淀粉勾芡，再放入鸡丝，撒入花椒粉翻炒均匀，淋上麻油，装盘即成。

特点：色泽红亮

口味：集麻，辣，咸，鲜于一体

Peppery Shredded Chicken

Ingredients：

250 grams (0.55 lb) chicken breast
150 grams (0.33 lb) bamboo shoots
500 grams (1 cup) cooking oil (only 1/5 to be consumed)
1 egg white
1 1/2 grams (1/4 tsp) salt
1 gram (1/4 tsp) MSG
75 grams (5 tbsp) water
12 grams (1 2/3 tbsp) dry cornstarch
10 grams (2 tsp) cooking wine
5 grams (1 tsp) sugar
2 dried red chilies
1 gram (1/5 tsp) pepper powder
20 grams (1 tbsp) soy sauce
5 grams (1/6 oz) scallions
5 grams (1/6 oz) ginger
5 grams (1 tsp) sesame oil

Directions：

1. Cut the chicken breast into shreds 5 cm (2 inches) long and 0.25 cm (0.1 inch) thick and wide. Place in a bowl. Add the salt, egg white and 10 g (1 1/2 tbsp) of dry cornstarch and mix well. Mix the remaining cornstarch with water. Cut the bamboo shoots into shreds similar to the chicken in size. Finely cut the scallions, chilies and chop the ginger.

2. Heat the oil over strong fire to 70-100℃ (160-210˚F) and slippery-fry the chicken shreds for 1-2 minutes. Put in a strainer to drain off the oil.

3. Put 50 g (3 1/2 tbsp) of oil in the wok and stir-fry the scallions, ginger and red chilies until they produce a strong aroma. Put in the bamboo shoots to quickly stir-fry by turning over several times. Add the cooking wine, water, soy sauce, sugar and MSG and bring to boil. Thicken the sauce with the mixture of cornstarch and water. Add the chicken shreds, sprinkle on the pepper powder and turn several times. Sprinkle on the sesame oil and serve.

Features：Shiny and brown in color.
Taste：Peppery, spicy, salty and refreshing all at the same time.

麻辣鸡丝
Peppery Shredded Chicken

香炸八块

主料：净膛童仔鸡1只（约600克）或肉用鸡腿500克

辅料：粳米粉150克

调料：油1000克（约耗100克）、鸡蛋1只、油咖喱15克、盐4克、味精2克、料酒20克

制作：①将鸡去头、颈、爪，鸡身从脊背处劈开，再剁成约4厘米见方的块，放入汤碗中，磕入鸡蛋，加盐、油咖喱、味精、料酒拌匀后腌制2小时，再放入粳米粉拌匀。

②炒锅置旺火上烧热，倒入油，烧到四成热时，放入鸡块，炸至断生捞出。油锅继续加热，待油温升到八成热时，将炸好的鸡块再炸一次至表皮呈金黄色，捞出，装盘即成。

特点：色泽金黄，外脆里嫩

口味：咸鲜适口

Crispy Chicken

Ingredients：

1 young chicken (about 600 g or 1.3 lb) with the inside removed. Alternatively 500 g (1.1 lb) of chicken legs

150 grams (0.33 lb) rice flour

1000 grams (2 cups) cooking oil (only 1/10 to be consumed)

1 egg

15 grams (1 1/2 tbsp) curry

4 grams (2/3 tsp) salt

2 grams (1/2 tsp) MSG

20 grams (1 2/3 tbsp) cooking wine

Directions：

1. Remove the head, neck and feet of the chicken. Cut the chicken open from the back and reduce into chunks about 4 cm (1.6 inches) long each side. Put in a large bowl. Add the egg, salt, curry, MSG and cooking wine to marinate for 2 hours. Now mix well with the rice flour.

2. Heat the oil in a wok over strong fire to 70-100℃ (160-210°F) and quickly deep-fry the chicken chunks. Take out and continue to heat the oil to 200-220℃ (390-430°F). Now deep-fry the chicken chunks again until they are golden yellow in color. Take out and drain off the oil. Dish is ready to serve.

Features：Golden yellow in color. Tender inside and crispy outside.

Taste：Salty to the right taste.

芝麻鸡排

主料：鸡脯肉 300 克

辅料：芝麻 100 克

调料：油 1000 克（约耗 50 克）、鸡蛋 1 只、油咖喱 2 克、盐 2 克、味精 1 克、干淀粉 25 克、料酒 10 克

制作：①将鸡脯肉切成厚 0.25 厘米的片，放入碗中，加油咖喱、盐、味精、料酒，磕入鸡蛋搅拌上劲加入干淀粉拌匀。芝麻炒熟。将浆好的鸡片平放在砧板上，然后在两面均匀地洒上芝麻，用手拍紧备用。

②炒锅置旺火上烧热，倒入油，烧到七成热时，放入鸡片炸熟捞出，锅继续加热，待油温升至八成热时，将炸好的鸡片再炸一次至金黄色捞出。

③将炸好的鸡排切成小块，装盘即成。

特点：香脆可口，外脆里嫩

口味：咸鲜适口

Sesame Chicken Fillet

Ingredients：

300 grams (0.66 lb) chicken breast
100 grams (0.22 lb) sesame
1000 grams (2 cups) cooking oil (only 1/20 to be consumed)
1 egg
2 grams (1/2 tsp) curry
1 gram (1/4 tsp) MSG
25 grams (2 1/4 tbsp) dry cornstarch
10 grams (2 tsp) cooking wine

Directions：

1. Cut the chicken breast into slices 0.25 cm (0.1 inch) thick, put in a bowl and add the curry, salt, MSG, cooking wine, egg and dry cornstarch. Mix well. Bake the sesame until it is done. Put the marinated chicken fillet on a board and dust sesame on both sides. Use hand to press in the sesame so as to make sure it will stay evenly on the chicken.

2. Heat the oil in a wok over strong fire to 180-200℃ (355-390˚F) and deep-fry the chicken fillets. Take out and bring the oil to 200-220℃ (390-430˚F). Now deep-fry the chicken slices again until they are golden yellow in color.

3. Cut the fillet into smaller sizes and place on a plate to serve.

Features：Crispy and fragrant.
Taste：Salty to the right taste.

芝麻鸡排
Sesame Chicken Fillet

香炸鸡球

主料：鸡脯肉 300 克

辅料：黄油 50 克、火腿 15 克、水发香菇 20 克、蒸发干贝 15 克、虾仁 20 克

调料：油 1000 克（约耗 50 克），鸡蛋 1 只、干淀粉 10 克、葱 10 克、盐 2 克、味精 1 克

制作：①将鸡脯肉斩成茸放入碗中，加盐，磕入鸡蛋搅拌上劲后，再放入淀粉拌匀备用。

②将黄油化开，火腿、香菇、干贝、虾仁、葱均切成末与黄油一起拌匀后放入冰箱，待凝结后搓成直径 1 厘米的小球备用。

③将拌好的鸡茸拍成若干个小饼，放入黄油球，搓成直径 2.5 厘米的球待用。

④炒锅置旺火上烧热，倒入油，烧至六成热时转改微火，将鸡球放入锅中炸熟，捞出，转旺火待油温升至八成热时，将炸好的鸡球再炸一次至金黄色，捞出装盘即成。

特点：外脆里嫩，馅心别有风味

口味：咸鲜适口

Fried Chicken Meatballs

Ingredients：

300 grams (0.66 lb) chicken breast
50 grams (0.11 lb) butter
15 grams (1/2 oz) ham
20 grams (2/3 oz) mushrooms already soaked in water
15 grams (1/2 oz) scallops
20 grams (2/3 oz) shelled shrimps
1000 grams (2 cups) cooking oil (only 1/20 to be consumed)
1 egg
10 grams (1 1/2 tsp) dry cornstarch
10 grams (1/3 oz) scallions
2 grams (1/3 tsp) salt
1 gram (1/4 tsp) MSG

Directions：

1. Grind the chicken breast and place in a bowl. Add the salt and egg and stir well until mixture becomes sticky. Add the dry cornstarch and mix well.

2. Let the butter melt and mix with the finely chopped ham, mushrooms, scallops, shrimps and scallions. Put the mixture in refrigerator to marinate in a cold temperature. When substance solidifies, shape it into small balls 1 cm (0.4 inch) in diameter.

3. Shape the ground chicken into several small flat cakes. Place the butter balls on top of them and roll up into balls 2. 5 cm (1 inch) in diameter for use later.

4. Heat the oil in a wok over strong fire to 135-170℃ (275-340˚F) and turn to low fire. Deep-fry the meatballs until they are done. Take out and bring the oil temperature up to 200-220℃ (390-430˚F). Deep-fry the meatballs again until they are brown in color. Take out and serve.

Features：Crispy outside and tender inside. The meatballs are particularly tasty with the filling of mixed ingredients.
Taste：Salty to the right taste.

香炸鸡球
Fried Chicken Meatballs

香炸仔鸡

主料：净膛童仔鸡 1 只（约 600 克）或肉用鸡腿 500 克

调料：油 1500 克（约耗 100 克）、酱油 15 克、蚝油 10 克、盐 3 克、味精 2 克、料酒 25 克、胡椒粉 1 克、葱段、姜片各 10 克。

制作：①将仔鸡去头、颈、爪，从背脊处劈开，用刀根斩断背、胸、腿的骨头，肉厚处也用刀根剁几下便于入味，放入碗中，加入酱油、蚝油、盐、料酒、胡椒粉、味精、葱段、姜片腌渍 1 小时左右。

②炒锅置旺火上烧热，倒入油，烧至八成热时，放入鸡炸至鸡皮上有小白点后转微火煨至熟透，捞出。

③油锅转旺火，待油温升至八成热时，放入鸡再炸一下，至表皮松脆，捞出，用刀剁成小块装盘即成。上桌时附加一碟芝麻盐佐食。

特点：色泽金黄，鸡皮香脆

口味：咸鲜适口

Deep-fried Tender Chicken

Ingredients：

1 young chicken (about 600 g or 1.3 lb) with the inside removed or alternatively 500 g (1.1 lb) chicken legs
1500 grams (3 cups) oil (only 1/15 to be consumed)
15 grams (1 3/4 tsp) soy sauce
10 grams (1 1/2 tsp) oyster sauce
3 grams (1/2 tsp) salt
2 grams (1/2 tsp) MSG
25 grams (1 3/4 tbsp) cooking wine
1 gram (1/5 tsp) pepper powder
10 grams (1/3 oz) sectioned scallions
10 grams (1/3 oz) sliced ginger
1 small plate of baked sesame mixed with salt

Directions：

1. Remove the head, neck and feet of the chicken. Cut open from the back and break the bones in the back, chest and legs. Where the meat is thick, make a few cuts for better absorption of the seasonings. Place in a large bowl. Add the soy sauce, oyster sauce, salt, cooking wine, pepper powder, MSG, scallions and ginger to marinate for 1 hour.

2. Heat the oil in a wok over a strong fire to 200-220℃ (390-430˚F) and deep-fry the chicken until bubbles appear on the skin. Turn to a low fire to simmer until the meat is done. Take out.

3. Turn the wok with the oil to a strong fire and, when the temperature rises to the previous height, deep-fry the chicken again until the skin becomes loose. Take out and cut into smaller chunks to serve. Put a small plate with a mixture of salt and baked sesame next to it to go with the chicken.

Features：Golden yellow in color and crispy.
Taste：Salty to the right taste.

香炸仔鸡
Deep-fried Tender Chicken

蚝油鸡球

主料：鸡脯肉 400 克

调料：油 500 克（实耗 100 克）、鸡蛋 1 只、干淀粉 15 克、蚝油 25 克、酱油 10 克、糖 15 克、味精 1 克、盐 3 克、清汤 75 克、料酒 5 克

制作：①将鸡脯肉斩成茸，放入碗中，加入淀粉 10 克和盐，磕入鸡蛋搅拌上劲，再搓成若干个直径 2 厘米的小球。余下的淀粉用水化开。

②炒锅置旺火上烧热，倒入油，烧至六成热时，将鸡球放入油锅中炸熟，捞出。

③锅留余油 25 克烧热，放入蚝油、酱油、糖、味精、料酒、清汤烧开后，倒入鸡球，用湿淀粉勾芡，翻炒均匀，淋上少许麻油，装盘即成。

特点：鸡球滑嫩，鲜香可口

口味：咸鲜适口

Chicken Meatballs with Oyster Sauce

Ingredients：
400 grams (0.88 lb) chicken breast
500 grams (1 cup) cooking oil (only 1/5 to be consumed)
1 egg
15 grams (1 3/4 tbsp) dry cornstarch
25 grams (1 1/2 tbsp) oyster sauce
10 grams (1 1/2 tsp) soy sauce
15 grams (1 tbsp) sugar
1 gram (1/4 tsp) MSG
3 grams (1/2 tsp) salt
5 grams (1 tsp) cooking wine
75 grams (5 tbsp) water

Directions：
1. Grind the chicken breast and place it in a bowl. Add 10 g (1 1/2 tbsp) of dry cornstarch, salt and egg, and stir until substance becomes sticky. Shape the mixture into small balls 2 cm (0.8 inch) in diameter. Mix the remaining cornstarch with water.

2. Heat the oil in a wok over a strong fire to 135-170℃ (275-340°F) and deep-fry the chicken balls until they are done.

3. Put 25 g (1 2/3 tbsp) of oil in the wok and add the oyster sauce, soy sauce, sugar, MSG, cooking wine and water, and bring to boil. Add the chicken balls and thicken the sauce with the mixture of cornstarch and water. Turn several times, sprinkle on a few drops of sesame oil and take out to serve.

Features: The chicken balls are slippery and taste really nice.
Taste: Salty and delicious to the right taste.

蚝油鸡球
Chicken Meatballs with Oyster Sauce

油泼鸡

主料：净膛仔鸡 1 只（约 600 克）

调料：油 1500 克（约耗 100 克）、酱油 30 克、辣酱油 30 克、味精 1 克、胡椒粉 1 克、葱、姜、蒜末各 5 克、料酒 50 克、糖 15 克、清汤 50 克

制作：①将仔鸡从脊背处劈开，用刀根斩断背、胸、腿骨，用酱油腌渍 15 分钟（如用肉用鸡腿在腿骨和肉厚的地方也要剁几下，以便入味及成熟）。

②炒锅置于旺火上烧热，倒入油，待油温升至七成热时，放入鸡，炸至鸡皮呈黄红色转微火，待鸡熟透时，捞出，用刀切成小块拼成鸡形置于盘中。

③锅内留余油 25 克烧热，放入葱、姜、蒜末，煸炒出香味，放入料酒、辣酱油、胡椒粉、清汤、糖、味精。烧开后泼于鸡上即成。

特点：色泽红亮，外脆里嫩

口味：酸甜适口，咸鲜微辣

Sizzling Chicken

Ingredients:

1 young chicken (about 600 grams or 1.3 lb)
1500 grams (3 cups) cooking oil (only 1/15 to be consumed)
30 grams (1 2/3 tbsp) soy sauce
30 grams (1 2/3 tbsp) spicy soy sauce
1 gram (1/4 tsp) MSG
1 gram (1/5 tsp) pepper powder
5 grams (1/6 oz) finely cut scallions
5 grams (1/6 oz) chopped ginger
5 grams (1/6 oz) chopped garlic
50 grams (3 1/3 tbsp) cooking wine
15 grams (1 tbsp) sugar
50 grams (3 tbsp) water

Directions:

1. Cut open the chicken from the back and break the bones in the back, chest and legs. Where the meat is thick, make a few cuts to better absorb the seasonings. Marinate in soy sauce for 15 minutes.

2. Heat the oil in a wok over strong fire to 180-200℃（355-390˚F）and deep-fry the chicken until the skin turns orange in color. Turn the fire to low to cook until the chicken is done. Take out, reduce to smaller chunks and put on a plate.

3. Put 25 g (1 2/3 tbsp) of oil in the wok and stir-fry the scallions, ginger and garlic until they produce a strong aroma. Add the cooking wine, spicy soy sauce, pepper powder, water, sugar and MSG, and bring to a boil. Sprinkle the sauce onto the chicken chunks.

Features: Shiny and brown in color. Crispy outside and tender inside.

Taste: Sweet and sour to the right taste. Salty and slightly spicy.

油泼鸡
Sizzling Chicken

东安仔鸡

主料：净膛仔鸡 1 只（约 600 克）

辅料：笋、胡萝卜、青椒各 50 克

调料：油 100 克、盐 3 克、味精 2 克、葱、姜丝各 10 克、干红辣椒 5 克、花椒末 1 克、麻油 5 克、醋 50 克、湿淀粉 20 克、料酒 20 克、清汤 125 克

制作：①锅内放入冷水置旺火上，放入鸡煮熟。捞出后斩去头、颈、爪，剖开膛剔去所有的骨头，顺丝切成 5 厘米长、1 厘米宽的条。笋、胡萝卜、青椒切条。干红辣椒切丝。

②锅置旺火上放入油，烧热，烹入鸡条、姜丝、干红辣椒丝，煸炒出香味，放入笋条、青椒条、胡萝卜条、料酒、醋、盐、花椒末继续煸炒，再放入清汤，烧开后加盖转小火微焖，收汁后放入葱丝，用湿淀粉勾芡，淋上麻油，装盘即成。

特点：色彩鲜艳

口味：咸鲜略酸

Andong-style Tender Chicken

Ingredients:

1 young chicken (about 600 g or 1.3 lb), inside removed
50 grams (0.11 lb) bamboo shoots
50 grams (0.11 lb) carrots
50 grams (0.11 lb) green peppers
100 grams (7 tbsp) cooking oil
3 grams (1/2 tsp) salt
2 grams (1/2 tsp) MSG
10 grams (1/3 oz) shredded scallion
10 grams (1/3 oz) shredded ginger
5 grams (1/6 oz) dried red chilies
1 gram (1/5 tsp) pepper powder
5 grams (1 tsp) sesame oil
50 grams (3 tbsp) vinegar
20 grams (1 tbsp) mixture of cornstarch and water
20 grams (1 1/3 tbsp) cooking wine
125 grams (7 2/3 tbsp) water

Directions:

1. Put cold water in a pot over a strong fire and submerge the chicken in the pot to cook until it is done. Remove the head, neck and feet. Cut open and remove all the bones. Cut the meat into strips along the grain 5 cm (1.6 inches) long and 1 cm (0.4 inch) wide. Cut the bamboo shoots, carrots and green peppers into strips too. Reduce the dried red chilies into shreds.

2. Heat the oil in a wok over strong fire to 135-170℃ (275-340°F) and stir-fry the chicken strips, ginger shreds and red chili shreds until they produce a distinctive aroma. Add the bamboo, carrots, green peppers, cooking wine, vinegar, salt and pepper powder, and continue to stir-fry for 1-2 minutes. Add the water and when it boils, turn to a low fire to simmer several minutes. When the liquid boils off somewhat and is reduced in quantity, add the scallions and the mixture of cornstarch and water. Sprinkle on the sesame oil and take out to serve.

Features: Beautiful in color.

Taste: Salty, slightly sour and refreshing.

松仁鸡卷

主料：鸡脯肉 200 克

辅料：鲜虾仁 150 克、松子仁 50 克

调料：油 500 克（实耗 100 克）、鸡蛋清 1 只、盐 4 克、味精 1 克、干淀粉 20 克

制作：①将鸡脯肉切成厚 0.2 厘米的片。虾仁斩成茸。松子仁炸熟后辗成末。

②鸡片放入碗中加 1 克盐和蛋清，搅拌上劲后放入 10 克干淀粉拌匀。虾茸内放入 2 克盐和味精搅拌上劲后放入松仁末拌匀。

③鸡片平放砧板上拍上干淀粉，放上虾茸，抹平后卷成直径 2 厘米左右的卷。

④炒锅置旺火上烧热，倒入油，待油温升至五成热时，放入鸡卷炸至断生，捞出后切成小段，装盘即成。

特点：鸡卷色白，香脆鲜嫩

口味：咸鲜适口

Chicken Rolls with Pine Nuts

Ingredients：
200 grams (0.44 lb) chicken breast
150 grams (0.33 lb) fresh shelled shrimps
50 grams (0.11 lb) shelled pine nuts
500 grams (1 cup) cooking oil (only 1/5 to be consumed)
1 egg white
4 grams (2/3 tsp) salt
1 gram (1/4 tsp) MSG
20 grams (2 tbsp) dry cornstarch

Directions：
1. Cut the chicken breast into slices 0.2 cm (0.08 inch) thick. Chop the shrimps into paste. Deep-fry the pine nuts and grind into powder.

2. Put the chicken slices in a bowl, add 1 g (1/6 tsp) of salt and the egg white, and mix well until substance becomes sticky. Add 10 g (1 1/2 tbsp) of dry cornstarch and mix evenly. Add 2 g (1/3 tsp) of salt and the MSG to the shrimp paste and mix until this becomes sticky. Put in the pine nut powder and mix well.

3. Place the chicken slices on a chopping board and with dust dry cornstarch. Place the shrimp paste on top and roll up into rolls 2 cm (0.8 inch) in diameter.

4. Heat the oil in a wok over strong fire to 110-135℃ (230-275°F) and deep-fry the chicken rolls until they are done. Take out and cut into short sections. Put on a plate and serve.

Features：White in color and tender and crispy to the bite.
Taste：Salty and delicious.

松仁鸡卷
Chicken Rolls with Pine Nuts

黄焖鸡

主料：净膛仔鸡1只（约600克）或肉用鸡腿600克

调料：油1000克（实耗100克）、酱油20克、糖25克、大料2只、葱段、姜片各10克、料酒10克、盐2克、清汤500克、麻油10克

制作：①仔鸡从脊背处剖开，用刀根将背骨、胸骨、腿骨斩断，用10克酱油在鸡身上抹匀。

②炒锅置旺火上烧热，倒入油，待油温升至八成热时，放入鸡炸至皮上起白泡捞出。

③锅内留油50克烧热，下葱段煸炒出香味，放入鸡、料酒、大料、酱油、糖、清汤、盐、姜片，用旺火烧开后转小火，加盖焖约30分钟，使其入味后转旺火收汁，待汤汁粘稠后，拣出大料，淋上麻油，装盘即成。

特点：色泽棕黄，鸡肉酥烂

口味：咸甜适口

Boiled Chicken in Brown Sauce

Ingredients：

1 young chicken (about 600 g or 1.3 lb) with the inside removed or alternatively 600 g of chicken legs
1000 grams (2 cups) cooking oil (only 1/10 to be consumed)
20 grams (1 tbsp) soy sauce
25 grams (1 3/4 tbsp) sugar
2 pieces of star anise
10 grams (1/3 oz) sectioned scallions
10 grams (1/3 oz) sliced ginger
10 grams (2 tsp) cooking wine
2 grams (1/3 tsp) salt
500 grams (1 cup) water
10 grams (2 tsp) sesame oil

Directions：

1. Cut the chicken open from the back, and break the bones in the back, chest and legs. Rub the chicken evenly with 10 g (1 1/2 tsp) of soy sauce.

2. Heat the oil in a wok over strong fire to 200-220℃ (390-430˚F) and deep-fry the chicken until white bubbles appear on the skin.

3. Put 50 g (7 tbsp) of oil in the wok and stir-fry the scallions until they produce a strong aroma. Put in the chicken, cooking wine, star anise, soy sauce, sugar, water, salt and ginger, and bring to boil. Turn down the fire until it is low. Put on the wok lid and simmer for 30 minutes. When the seasonings are absorbed, turn to a strong fire to boil off some of the liquid. Once the mixture becomes sticky, take out the star anise, sprinkle on sesame oil and put on a serving plate.

Features：Brown in color, chicken is really soft.
Taste：Salty and sweet to the right taste.

砂锅鸡块

主料：鸡腿 350 克

辅料：笋 150 克、油菜心 20 克

调料：油 10 克、盐 5 克、味精 2 克、姜块 15 克、葱段 5 克、清汤 750 克、料酒 10 克

制作：①将鸡腿斩成 3 厘米见方的块，放入开水锅内煮出浮沫，捞出，洗去白沫，控干水。笋切成滚刀块。油菜洗净。

②取砂锅置于灶上，将笋块放在底部，洗净的鸡块置于笋块上，加清汤、盐、味精、油菜心、葱段、姜块（拍松），用旺火烧开后撇去浮沫，淋上油转小火焖 2 小时左右。火的大小以不翻滚只有少数小气泡上浮为宜。食时拣去葱段、姜块。

特点：汤汁清香，鸡肉酥烂脱骨

口味：咸鲜适口

Stewed Chicken Chunks in Earthen Pot

Ingredients：
350 grams (0.77 lb) chicken legs
150 grams (0.33 lb) bamboo shoots
20 grams (2/3 oz) tender green vegetables
10 grams (2 tsp) cooking oil
5 grams (5/6 tsp) salt
2 grams (1/2 tsp) MSG
15 grams (1/2 oz) ginger cubes
5 grams (1/6 oz) sectioned scallions
750 grams (1 1/2 cups) water
10 grams (2 tsp) cooking wine

Directions：
1. Cut the chicken legs into squares 3 cm (1.2 inches) long on each side and quick boil in hot water. Take out, wash off the surface foam and drain off the water. Cut the bamboo shoots into small chunks.

2. Place an earthen pot on the stove. Put the bamboo chunks at the bottom topped with chicken chunks. Add water, salt, MSG, green vegetables, scallions, and ginger cubes (previously crushed) to heat over a strong fire. Skim off the foam, sprinkle on the oil and simmer over a low fire for about 2 hours. Maintain the fire at such heat so that the soup bubbles but does not actively boil. Before serving, pick out the scallions and ginger.

Features：The soup is refreshing and the meat entirely falls off the bones.
Taste：Salty and delicious.

砂锅鸡块
Stewed Chicken Chunks in Earthen Pot

汽锅清炖鸡翅

主料： 鸡翅 750 克

辅料： 火腿 75 克、笋 50 克

调料： 油 10 克、盐 4 克、味精 2 克、葱段 5 克、姜块 10 克（拍松）、料酒 10 克

制作： ①鸡翅从关节处斩断，取翅根和中段，放入开水锅内煮出浮沫，捞出，洗去白沫控干水。火腿和笋均切成 2 厘米宽、4 厘米长、0.2 厘米厚的片。

②将鸡翅放入汽锅内，加盐、味精、料酒、火腿片和笋片，再加葱、姜、油，加盖后隔水炖 1 小时左右即可。上桌时再开盖，拣去葱、姜，以保证鸡的香味纯正。

特点： 鸡肉香醇，原汁原味

口味： 咸香适口

Chicken Wings in Steam Pot

Ingredients：
750 grams (1.65 lb) chicken wings
75 grams (0.165 lb or 2 1/2 oz) ham
50 grams (0.11 lb) bamboo shoots
10 grams (2 tsp) cooking oil
4 grams (2/3 tsp) salt
2 grams (1/2 tsp) MSG
5 grams (1/6 oz) sectioned scallions
10 grams (1/3 oz) crushed ginger cubes
10 grams (2 tsp) cooking wine

Directions：
1. Divide the wings from the joints. Don't use the wing tip sections, but boil the other two sections of the wings in hot water until foams appear. Take out, wash off the foam and drain off the water. Cut both the ham and bamboo shoots into slices 4 cm (1.6 inches) long, 2 cm (0.8 inch) wide and 0.2 cm (0.08 inch) thick.

2. Put the wings in an earthen steam pot. Add salt, MSG, cooking wine, ham, bamboo shoots, scallions, ginger and oil, and put on the lid to simmer for about 1 hour. Don't take off the lid until starting to serve, and pick out the scallions and ginger to ensure the pure taste of the chicken.

Features： The chicken meat is simply delicious and the soup is richly refreshing.
Taste： Salty and delicious.

红煨鸡腿

主料：鸡腿 10 只（约 750 克）

调料：油 100 克、蕃茄酱 125 克、洋葱丝 50 克、辣酱油 20 克、糖 75 克、盐 2 克、味精 2 克、料酒 10 克、清汤 400 克

制作：①锅内放入冷水置于旺火上，放入鸡腿烧开，煮出血沫，捞出后放入冷水中洗净，控干水。

②锅置旺火上烧热放入油，投入洋葱丝煸炒出香味，放入蕃茄酱、糖、盐、味精、辣酱油、清汤、鸡腿，加料酒烧开后转小火焖 30 分钟，再转旺火收至汤汁粘稠后，装盘即成。

特点：色泽红亮，鸡肉香嫩

口味：咸中带甜酸

Braised Chicken Legs

Ingredients:
10 chicken legs (about 750 g or 1.65 lb)
100 grams (7 tbsp) cooking oil
125 grams (11 tbsp) ketchup
50 grams (0.11 lb) shredded onion
20 grams (1 tbsp) spicy soy sauce
75 grams (5 1/4 tbsp) sugar
2 grams (1/3 tsp) salt
2 grams (1/2 tsp) MSG
10 grams (2 tsp) cooking wine
400 grams (4/5 cup) water

Directions:

1. Boil the chicken legs in a pot until there is foam on top of the water. Take out, wash clean in cold water and drain off the water.

2. Heat a wok. Put in the oil and stir-fry the onion until it gives a strong aroma. Add ketchup, sugar, salt, MSG, spicy soy sauce, water, chicken legs and cooking wine, and bring to boil. Turn to low fire to simmer for 30 minutes and use strong fire to reduce the amount of liquid until it becomes sticky. Take out and serve.

Features: The meat is shiny brown and delicious.
Taste: Salty with a slight sweet and sour taste.

红煨鸡腿
Braised Chicken Legs

红烧鸡块

主料：鸡腿 500 克

辅料：土豆 200 克

调料：油 500 克（约耗 100 克）、酱油 50 克、糖 20 克、味精 2 克、干淀粉 2 克、葱段 15 克、姜片 10 克、清汤 250 克、料酒 10 克

制作：①鸡腿斩成 4 厘米见方的块。土豆切成滚刀块，用清水浸泡备用。淀粉加 25 克水溶解开。

②锅置旺火上烧热，放入油，待油温升至八成热时下鸡块炸至皮上起白泡捞出。土豆放入油锅中炸至金黄色捞出，控净油。

③锅留余油 25 克烧热，放入葱段、姜片，煸炒出香味，倒入鸡块、料酒、酱油、糖、清汤，烧开后转小火焖 20 分钟，倒入土豆块继续焖 15 分钟，再转大火收稠汤汁，用湿淀粉勾芡，淋上麻油，装盘即可。

特点：鲜香嫩滑，色泽红亮

口味：甜中带咸，咸中带鲜

Braised Chicken Chunks with Brown Sauce

Ingredients：
500 grams (1.1 lb) chicken legs
200 grams (0.44 lb) potatoes
500 grams (1 cup) cooking oil (only 1/5 to be consumed)
50 grams (2 2/3 tbsp) soy sauce
20 grams (1 1/2 tbsp) sugar
2 grams (1/2 tsp) MSG
2 grams (1 tsp) dry cornstarch
15 grams (1/2 oz) sectioned scallions
10 grams (1/3 oz) sliced ginger
250 grams (1/2 cup) water
10 grams (2 tsp) cooking wine

Directions：
1. Cut the chicken legs into squares 4 cm (1.6 inches) long each side. Cut the potatoes into chunks a bit smaller than the chicken and soak in water. Mix the cornstarch with 25 g (1 2/3 tbsp) of water.

2. Heat the oil in a wok to 200-220℃ (390-430°F) and deep-fry the chicken until white bubbles appear on the skin. Take out and drain off the oil. Deep-fry the potatoes until they are golden yellow. Take out and drain in a strainer.

3. Put 25 g (1 2/3 tbsp) of oil in the wok and stir-fry the scallions and ginger until they produce a strong aroma. Add the chicken chunks, cooking wine, soy sauce, sugar and water, and bring to boil. Turn to low fire to simmer for about 20 minutes. Put in the potato chunks and continue to simmer for 15 minutes. Now turn to strong fire to reduce the amount of liquid until it becomes sticky. Use the mixture of cornstarch and water to thicken the soup. Sprinkle on a few drops of sesame oil and serve.

Features：Tender and slippery, the chicken shows an inviting red shiny color.

Taste：Sweet with a salty taste. Delicious indeed.

红烧鸡块
Braised Chicken Chunks with Brown Sauce

芙蓉鸡片

主料：鸡脯肉 200 克

辅料：鸡蛋清 5 只

调料：油 500 克（约耗 100 克）、盐 2 克、味精 1 克、清汤 125 克、青椒、胡萝卜各 20 克、湿淀粉 20 克

制作：①将鸡脯肉切成片，用 1 克盐、半个蛋清搅拌上劲后，加入 5 克湿淀粉拌匀备用。余下的蛋清内加入清汤 75 克、盐 0.5 克、味精 0.5 克和湿淀粉 8 克打散备用。青椒、胡萝卜均切成菱形片。

②炒锅置旺火上烧热，倒入油，待油温升至四成热时，倒入蛋液，锅离火并不停搅动，直至蛋清凝结膨起，宛如怒放的芙蓉。如不膨起可将锅再置旺火上以增高油温直至蛋清全部膨起，倒入漏勺内控净油后倒入盘中。

③原锅置火上，再将油倒回锅内，烧至四成热时，放入鸡片滑开炒熟，倒入漏勺中，控净油。

④锅留余油 25 克烧热，放入青椒片、胡萝卜片、盐、味精，翻炒数下，用湿淀粉勾芡，倒入炸好的蛋清和鸡片翻炒均匀，装盘即成。

特点：色泽洁白，入口嫩滑

口味：咸鲜适口

Sliced Chicken with Egg White

Ingredients：

200 grams (0.44 lb) chicken breast
5 eggs (only use the egg white)
500 grams (1 cup) cooking oil (only 1/5 to be consumed)
2 grams (1/3 tsp) salt
1 gram (1/4 tsp) MSG
125 grams (7 2/3 tbsp) water
20 grams (2/3 oz) green peppers
20 grams (2/3 oz) carrots
20 grams (2 tbsp) mixture of cornstarch and water

Directions：

1. Cut the chicken breast into slices and mix with 1 g (1/6 tsp) of salt, half of 1 egg white and 5 g (1 tsp) mixture of cornstarch and water. All the rest of the egg whites are mixed with 75 g (5 tbsp) of water, 1/2 g (1/12 tsp) of salt, 1/2 g (1/8 tsp) of MSG and 8 g (1 1/2 tsp) of mixture of cornstarch and water. Cut the green peppers and carrots into small diamond shapes.

2. Heat oil in a wok over a strong fire to 70-100℃ (160-210°F) and add the mixture of egg white and other ingredients. Hold the wok above the fire and keep turning until the egg white solidifies and pops up like blossoming hibiscus flowers. If it does not pop up, put the wok back on the fire to increase the temperature until all the egg white rises. Put in a strainer to drain off the oil and then onto a plate.

3. Put the oil back into the wok and bring it to 70-100℃ (160-210°F) to slippery-fry the chicken slices until they are done. Put in a strainer to drain off the oil.

4. Keep 25 g (1 2/3 tbsp) of oil in the wok. Add the green pepper, carrot, salt and MSG, and turn several times. Use the remaining mixture of cornstarch and water to thicken the liquid. Put in the fried egg white and mix evenly with the chicken slices. Put on a plate to serve.

Features：Pure white in color and slippery to the bite.
Taste：Salty and delicious.

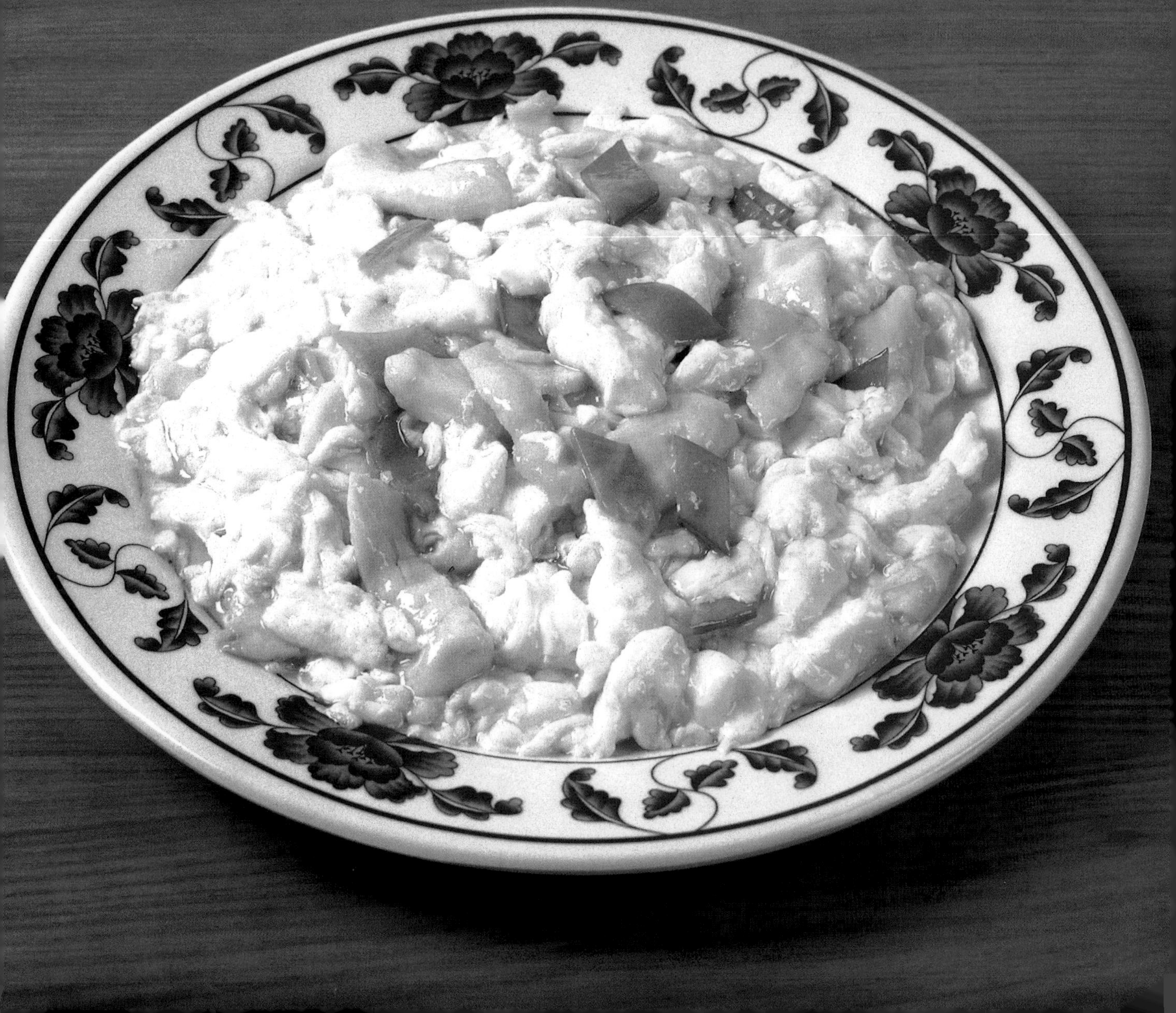

芙蓉鸡片
Sliced Chicken with Egg White

辣子鸡丁

主料：鸡脯肉 300 克

辅料：笋 150 克

调料：油 500 克（实耗 100 克）、盐 2 克、味精 2 克、酱油 20 克、糖 10 克、水泡红辣椒 50 克、葱、姜末各 5 克、干淀粉 3 克、湿淀粉 25 克、鸡蛋清 1 只、清汤 50 克

制作：①将鸡脯肉切成 1.5 厘米见方的丁，放入碗内，加 1 克盐和蛋清搅拌上劲后放入干淀粉拌匀备用。笋切 1 厘米见方的丁。红辣椒切 1 厘米长的段。

②取 1 小碗放入清汤、酱油、糖、味精、湿淀粉兑成芡汁。

③锅放旺火上烧热，倒入油，烧至四成热时倒入鸡丁滑炒至熟，倒入漏勺中控净油。

④锅留余油 50 克，加红辣椒用小火煸炒至油红，放入葱姜末、笋丁，煸炒几下，倒入鸡丁一起翻炒，加芡汁不停地煸炒，直至芡汁粘稠，均匀地包裹住鸡丁、笋丁，即可装盘。

特点：色泽红亮，辣而不辛

口味：咸鲜适口

Diced Chicken with Green Pepper

Ingredients：
300 grams (0.66 lb) chicken breast
150 grams (0.33 lb) bamboo shoots
500 grams (1 cup) cooking oil (only 1/5 to be consumed)
2 grams (1/3 tsp) salt
2 grams (1/2 tsp) MSG
20 grams (1 tbsp) soy sauce
10 grams (2 tsp) sugar
50 grams (0.11 lb) red chilies previously soaked in water
5 grams (1/6 oz) finely cut scallions
5 grams (1/6 oz) chopped ginger
3 grams (1 1/2 tsp) dry cornstarch
25 grams (2 1/3 tbsp) mixture of cornstarch and water
1 egg white
50 grams (3 tbsp) water

Directions：
1. Cut the chicken breast into dices 1.5 cm ((0.6 inch) long on each side and place in a bowl. Add 1 g (1/6 tsp) of salt, egg white and dry cornstarch, and mix well. Cut the bamboo shoots into dices 1 cm (0.4 inch) long on each side and reduce the red chilies into 1 cm (0.4 inch) long sections.

2. Put the water, soy sauce, sugar, MSG and mixture of cornstarch and water in a bowl to make a paste.

3. Heat the oil in a wok over strong fire to 70-100℃ (160-210˚F) and slippery-fry the chicken dices until they are done. Take out and drain off the oil.

4. Keep 50 g (3 1/2 tbsp) of oil in the wok and stir-fry the red chilies until the oil changes into a red color. Add the scallions, ginger and bamboo shoots, and stir-fry by turning several times. Add the chicken dices and turn several more times. Thicken the sauce with the mixture of cornstarch and water until the thickened sauce wraps around the chicken and bamboo evenly. Now serve.

Features：Shiny red in color, spicy but delicious.
Taste：Salty to the right taste.

辣子鸡丁
Diced Chicken with Green Pepper

白果烧鸡

主料：净膛仔鸡 1 只（约 600 克）

辅料：白果肉 200 克

调料：油 1000 克（油约耗 100 克）、酱油 75 克、盐 2 克、味精 2 克、料酒 10 克、糖 25 克、葱段 15 克、清汤 500 克、湿淀粉 10 克

制作：①仔鸡去头、爪，斩成 3 厘米见方的块，用酱油 25 克腌渍 15 分钟。

②锅置旺火上，倒入油，烧至八成热时，下鸡块炸至色红皮皱，捞出。油锅内放入白果肉炸至金黄色捞出。

③锅留余油 25 克烧热，下葱段略炒，放入鸡块、料酒、酱油、盐、味精、清汤，烧开后放入白果肉转小火焖约 30 分钟，收汁。

④待汁快干时用湿淀粉勾芡，淋上少许麻油，装盘即成。

特点：色泽淡红，白果香糯

口味：咸鲜适口

Stewed Chicken with Gingko Fruit

Ingredients:

1 young chicken (about 600 g or 1.3 lb), inside removed
200 grams (0.44 lb) gingko fruit
1000 grams (2 cups) cooking oil (only 1/10 to be consumed)
75 grams (4 tbsp) soy sauce
2 grams (1/3 tsp) salt
2 grams (1/2 tsp) MSG
10 grams (2 tsp) cooking wine
25 grams (1 3/4 tbsp) sugar
15 grams (1/2 oz) sectioned scallions
500 grams (1 cup) water
10 grams (2 tsp) mixture of cornstarch and water

Directions:

1. Remove the head, neck and feet of the chicken and cut into square chunks 3 cm (1.2 inches) long on each side. Marinate with 25 g (1 1/2 tbsp) of soy sauce for 15 minutes.

2. Heat the oil in a wok over strong fire to 200-220°C (390-430°F) and deep-fry the chicken chunks until the skin turns brown in color and wrinkles. Take out and drain off the oil. Deep-fry the gingko fruit until each one is golden yellow in color.

3. Keep 25 g (1 2/3 tbsp) of oil in the wok and stir-fry the scallions for 10-20 seconds. Add the chicken, cooking wine, soy sauce, salt, MSG and water, and bring to boil. Put in the gingko fruit and turn fire to low to simmer for 30 minutes. Use strong fire to reduce the amount of liquid.

4. Before the liquid dries up, put in the mixture of cornstarch and water and sprinkle on a few drops of sesame oil. The dish is now ready to serve.

Features: Light red in color. The gingko fruit, with a soft texture, gives a strong and fragrant aroma.
Taste: Salty and delicious.

白果烧鸡
Stewed Chicken with Gingko Fruit

锅烧鸡

主料：净膛仔鸡1只

辅料：面粉100克、鸡蛋2只

调料：油1000克（约耗50克）、盐5克、味精1克、料酒5克、白糖5克、葱、姜末各10克

制作：①将鸡去掉头、颈、爪，从脊背剖开放入盆内用3克盐搓匀，再放料酒、味精、白糖、葱姜末腌2小时。
②锅内放入冷水置旺火上，将鸡煮熟捞出，晾凉后，剔去所有的骨头。

③将鸡蛋磕入碗内打散，加入面粉、2克盐和水，调成糊，均匀地抹在鸡身上。
④锅置旺火上，放入油，待油温升至八成热时放入鸡，炸至面糊凝结后，转小火炸至金黄色，捞出控净油，切成小块装盘。花椒盐装入小碟随鸡肉一同上桌。

特点：色泽金黄，香松脆酥

口味：咸鲜适口

Deep-fried Boneless Chicken

Ingredients：

1 young chicken (about 600 g or 1.3 lb), inside removed
100 grams (0.22 lb) wheat flour
2 eggs
1000 grams (2 cups) cooking oil (only 1/20 to be consumed)
5 grams (5/6 tsp) salt
1 gram (1/4 tsp) MSG
5 grams (1 tsp) cooking wine
5 grams (1 tsp) sugar
10 grams (1/3 oz) finely cut scallions
10 grams (1/3 oz) chopped ginger

Directions：

1. Remove the head, neck and feet of the chicken. Cut open from the back and put in a basin to rub evenly with 3 g (1/2 tsp) of salt. Add the cooking wine, MSG, sugar, scallions and ginger to marinate for 2 hours.

2. Heat cold water in a pot over strong fire and boil the chicken until it is done. Take out and drain off the water. Remove all the bones.

3. Whip the eggs in a bowl. Add the flour, 2 g (1/3 tsp) of salt and the water to make a paste, and evenly rub the paste on the now boneless chicken.

4. Heat the oil in a wok over strong fire to 200-220℃ (390-430°F) and deep-fry the chicken until the flour paste solidifies. Turn to a low fire to continue to deep-fry until the chicken is golden yellow in color. Take out and drain off the oil. Cut into small chunks to serve along with a small plate of baked and ground pepper powder mixed with salt.

Features：Golden yellow in color, it is soft and crispy.
Taste：Salty and delicious.

锅烧鸡
Deep-fried Boneless Chicken

扣鸡

主料：净膛鸡1只（约600克）

辅料：笋100克

调料：油25克、盐4克、味精1克、清汤100克、葱末10克

制作：①锅内放入冷水置旺火上，放入鸡煮熟，捞出晾凉，斩去头、颈、爪。笋切块。

②将鸡斩成长5厘米、宽1厘米的块。皮朝下码放于碗中，中央放上笋块，加盐、味精、清汤上笼蒸约30分钟，取出，将汤滗入另一碗中备用。鸡扣于盘中。

③锅置火上，放入油烧热，烹入葱末炒出香味倒入鸡汤，烧开后淋于鸡身上即可。

特点：葱香笋鲜，鸡肉酥烂脱骨

口味：咸鲜适口

Stewed Chicken with Bamboo Shoots

Ingredients：

1 young chicken (about 600 g or 1.3 lb), inside removed
100 grams (0.22 lb) bamboo shoots
25 grams (1 2/3 tbsp) cooking oil
4 grams (2/3 tsp) salt
1 gram (1/4 tsp) MSG
100 grams (6 tbsp) water
10 grams (1/3 oz) finely cut scallions

Directions：

1. Put cold water in a pot and heat over a strong fire. Put in the chicken and boil until it is done. Take out and let it cool off. Cut off the head, neck and feet of the chicken. Cut the bamboo shoots into small chunks.

2. Cut the chicken into chunks 5 cm (2 inches) long and 1 cm (0.4 inch) wide. Place in a large bowl with the skin side down. Put the bamboo shoots on top of the chicken. Add the salt, MSG and water to steam for 30 minutes. Take out and pour the liquid into another bowl for use later. Put the chicken onto a plate by turning the large bowl upside down.

3. Heat the oil and stir-fry the scallions until they produce a strong aroma. Pour in the chicken-soup liquid. When it boils, sprinkle onto the chicken chunks.

Features: The scallion is fragrant and the bamboo is refreshing. The chicken meat is really soft.

Taste: Salty to the right taste.

扣鸡
Steamed Chicken with Bamboo Shoots

清炖童子鸡

主料：净膛仔鸡 1 只（约 600 克）

辅料：火腿 100 克、笋 100 克、小菜心 10 棵

调料：油 50 克、盐 4 克、味精 2 克、清汤 1000 克、葱、姜各 5 克

制作：①锅内放入冷水置旺火上，放入鸡煮出血沫，捞出洗净。火腿和笋切片。葱切段备用。

②取砂锅一只，将鸡腹朝上放入砂锅中，加清汤、盐、味精、油、葱段、姜块（拍松），将火腿片、笋片排列在鸡上，加盖后上笼蒸 2 小时。

③取出砂锅去盖，菜心用开水焯一下放在鸡的两边，将砂锅置在小火上烧开即成。

特点：酥烂脱骨，鸡形不变，原汁原味

口味：咸鲜适口

Stewed Tender Chicken

Ingredients：
1 young chicken (about 600 g or 1.3 lb), inside removed
100 grams (0.22 lb) ham
100 grams (0.22 lb) bamboo shoots
10 pieces of tender green vegetables
50 grams (3 1/2 tbsp) cooking oil
4 grams (2/3 tsp) salt
2 grams (1/2 tsp) MSG
1000 grams (2 cups) water
5 grams (1/6 oz) sectioned scallions
5 grams (1/6 oz) crushed ginger chunks

Directions：
1. Put cold water in a pot and heat over a strong fire. Put in the chicken and boil until blood comes out in the form of foam. Take out and wash clean. Cut the ham and bamboo shoots into slices.

2. Put the chicken with the belly up in an earthen pot. Add the water, salt, MSG, cooking oil, scallions and ginger in the pot. Place the bamboo shoots and ham slices on top of the chicken. Put on the lid and steam the earthen pot with the chicken in it for 2 hours.

3. Take the earthen pot out of the steamer. Remove the lid and place the green vegetables that have been previously quick-boiled in water on both sides of the chicken. Put the earthen pot on small fire and bring the dish to boil. It is ready to serve.

Features： The meat is so soft that it separates from the bones without any change in the shape of a whole chicken.

Taste： Salty and delicious.

清炖童仔鸡
Steamed Tender Chicken

烤鸡

主料：净膛嫩母鸡一只（约 1250 克）

辅料：香菇 20 克、笋 20 克、水发莲子 20 克、酱瓜 20 克、鲜百合 15 克、鲜虾仁 20 克、干贝 15 克、熟火腿 30 克、猪网油 2 张（猪腹内网状隔膜）

调料：油 25 克、甜面酱 15 克、葱、姜汁各 20 克、糖 2.5 克、盐 2 克、味精 1.5 克、料酒 20 克、清汤 10 克、饴糖水 2000 克

制作：①炒锅置旺火烧热，倒入油，待油温升至 4 成热时放入甜面酱、葱姜汁、糖、盐、味精、料酒、清汤，烧开后熄火，制成甜酱汁待用。干贝用温水发好。将香菇、笋、莲子、百合洗净。

②将鸡洗净控干水，将甜酱汁倒入鸡腹内放入盆中腌渍 30 分钟，倒出。

③将香菇、笋、酱瓜、百合、虾仁、干贝、火腿均切成丁。

④炒锅置旺火上，倒入甜酱汁，加入莲子及各种丁翻炒收汁后制成馅，填入鸡腹内，用针线将鸡腹口缝合后浸入饴糖水中上色。

⑤将鸡取出用猪网油包起来，上烤箱烧烤 30 分钟。烤时要不停地翻动，至鸡皮呈酱红色即可。

特点：嫩香鲜肥

口味：咸鲜适口，回味带甜

Roast Chicken

Ingredients：

1 tender hen (about 1250 g or 2.75 lb), inside removed
20 grams (2/3 oz) mushrooms
20 grams (2/3 oz) bamboo shoots
20 grams (2/3 oz) lotus seeds previously soaked in water
20 grams (2/3 oz) pickled cucumbers
15 grams (1/2 oz) fresh lilies
20 grams (2/3 oz) shelled fresh shrimps
15 grams (1/2 oz) scallops
30 grams (1 oz) cooked ham
25 grams (1 2/3 tbsp) cooking oil
15 grams (1 3/4 tsp) sweet soy bean paste
20 grams (2/3 oz) scallion juice (from soaking chopped scallions)
20 grams (2/3 oz) ginger juice (from soaking chopped ginger)
2 1/2 grams (2/5-3/5 tsp) sugar
2 grams (1/3 tsp) salt
1 1/2 grams (1/3 tsp) MSG
20 grams (1 2/3 tbsp) cooking wine
10 grams (2 tsp) water
2000 grams (4 cups) mixture of water with maltose sugar

Directions：

1. Heat the oil in a wok over strong fire to 70-100℃ (160-210°F) and add the sweet soy bean paste, scallion juice and ginger juice, sugar, salt, MSG, cooking wine and water, and bring to a boil. Turn off the fire and keep the sauce for later use.

2. Wash the chicken clean and drain off the water. Put the sauce into the chicken belly. Place the chicken in a basin to marinate for 30 minutes. Pour out the sauce.

3. Cut the mushrooms, bamboo shoots, cucumbers, lilies, shrimps, scallops and ham into small dices.

4. Heat the wok, pour in the sauce, add the lotus seed and the mixture of dices, and keep turning until the sauce is absorbed. Use the mixture as stuffing to put into the chicken belly. Sow up the belly and soak the chicken in the mixture of water with maltose sugar for coloring.

5. Take out the chicken, rub oil on it and put in an oven to roast for 30 minutes. It has to be kept turning in the oven until the skin turns brown.

Features：Tender and juice.
Taste：Salty and delicious with a slight sweet touch.

烤鸡
Roast Chicken

葱爆鸭丝

主料：鸭脯肉 250 克

辅料：笋 20 克，葱 50 克

调料：油 500 克（实耗 75 克）、盐 4 克、味精 2 克、料酒 5 克、干淀粉 2 克、清汤 50 克

制作：①将鸭脯肉切成长 5 厘米、宽 0.5 厘米、厚 0.5 厘米的丝。笋切成长 3 厘米、宽 0.3 厘米、厚 0.3 厘米的丝。葱切成 3 厘米的段。盐、味精、料酒、清汤、淀粉放入碗中调合成芡汁。

②炒锅置旺火上烧热，倒入油，烧至五成热时，放入鸭丝滑炒至断生，倒入漏勺中，控净油。

③锅内留余油 25 克烧热，放入葱段、笋丝煸炒出香味，倒入鸭丝及调好的芡汁翻炒均匀，淋上少许麻油，装盘即成。

特点：葱香肉嫩

口味：咸鲜

Quick-fried Shredded Duck with Scallions

Ingredients：

250 grams (0.55 lb) duck breast
20 grams (2/3 oz) bamboo shoots
50 grams (0.11 lb) scallions
500 grams (1 cup) oil (only 75 g or 5 tbsp to be consumed)
4 grams (2/3 tsp) salt
2 grams (1/2 tsp) MSG
5 grams (1 tsp) cooking wine
2 grams (1 tsp) dry cornstarch
50 grams (6 tbsp) water

Directions：

1. Cut the duck breast into shreds 5 cm (2 inches) long and 0.5 cm (0.2 inch) thick and wide. Cut the bamboo shoots into shreds 3 cm (1.2 inches) long and 0.3 cm (0.12 inch) thick and wide. Cut the scallions into sections 3 cm (1.2 inches) long. Put the salt, MSG, cooking wine, water and cornstarch in a bowl to make a paste.

2. Heat the oil in a wok over strong fire to 110-135℃ (230-275˚F) and quickly slippery-fry the duck shreds. Put in a strainer to drain off the oil.

3. Keep 25 g (1 2/3 tbsp) of oil in the wok and put in the scallion and bamboo shreds to stir-fry until they produce a distinctive aroma. Add the duck shreds and the pre-prepared paste to evenly turn several times. Sprinkle on a few drops of sesame oil and it is ready to serve.

Features：The scallion has a strong aroma and the duck meat is tender.

Taste：Salty and delicious.

葱爆鸭丝
Quick-fried Shredded Duck with Scallions

香酥鸭

主料：净膛鸭 1 只（约 1200 克）

调料：油 2000 克（约耗 50 克）、盐 10 克、料酒 15 克、味精 2 克、丁香 3 粒、花椒 5 克、桂皮 25 克、大料 4 只、葱段、姜片各 5 克、干淀粉 25 克、麻油 10 克

制作：①将鸭掌、翅尖剁去，剪去鸭臊（即鸭的尾部），然后洗净，将鸭控去水后放入容器内。将淀粉调成糊备用。把葱、姜、盐、丁香、花椒、桂皮、大料拌均，撒在鸭体内外腌渍 2 小时。撒上味精，然后上笼蒸至酥烂，取出晾凉。拣去葱、姜及香料。

②锅置旺火上烧热加入油，烧至八成热时，把鸭体抹上薄薄的一层淀粉糊，放入油锅中炸至金黄色，捞出控净油，斩成块装盘，淋上麻油即成。

特点：色泽金黄，脆酥肥嫩，五香味浓

口味：咸鲜适口

Crispy Duck

Ingredients：

1 duck (1200 g or 2.6 lb) with the insides removed
2000 grams (4 cups) cooking oil (only 1/40 to be consumed)
10 grams (1 2/3 tsp) salt
2 grams (1/2 tsp) MSG
15 grams (1 tbsp) cooking wine
3 grains of clove seeds
5 grams (1/6 oz) Chinese prickly ash
25 grams (4/5 oz) cassia bark
4 pieces of star anise
5 grams (1/6 oz) sectioned scallions
5 grams (1/6 oz) sliced ginger
25 grams (2 1/3 tbsp) dry cornstarch
10 grams (2 tsp) sesame oil

Directions：

1. Remove the webs, tips of wings and tail of the duck, wash clean and drain off the water. Put in a basin. Add water to the cornstarch to make paste for later use. Mix scallions, ginger, salt, clove seeds, Chinese prickly ash, cassia bark and star anise, and put inside the duck to marinate for 2 hours. Sprinkle on the MSG and steam the duck until its meat becomes really soft. Take duck out and cool off. Pick out the scallions, ginger and other spices.

2. Heat the oil in a wok over strong fire to 200-220℃ (390-430°F). Rub the duck with a thin layer of the cornstarch paste and deep-fry it until it is golden yellow in color. Take out and drain off the oil. Cut into chunks, place on a plate and sprinkle on the sesame oil.

Features：Golden yellow in color, rich but not greasy, and nicely flavored.

Taste：Salty to the right taste.

香酥鸭
Crispy Duck

姆油鸭

主料：净膛鸭 1 只（约 1200 克）

辅料：冬笋 25 克，小菜心 10 棵

调料：油 50 克、酱油 150 克、料酒 50 克、白糖 20 克、麻油 10 克、葱 50 克、姜 10 克、清汤 1000 克

制作：①葱切段，姜切片。鸭剪去掌和鸭臊，鸭头用翅膀夹紧，放入开水锅内煮出血沫，捞出洗净。鸭腹向下放入砂锅内，旁边放上葱段 10 克、姜片和笋。
②炒锅放入清汤置旺火上加酱油、糖、料酒烧沸，撇去浮沫，倒入砂锅内盖上盖。然后将砂锅置旺火上，烧开后转小火烧 3 小时左右，至鸭烂。
③拣去葱、姜将鸭身翻至鸭腹向上，取出笋切成片，小菜心入开水锅内焯熟，与笋片一起放在鸭腹上。
④炒锅置火上加入油烧热，投入 40 克葱段，熬黄后浇在鸭身上，淋上麻油即成。

特点：鸭形丰满，酥烂脱骨，肥而不腻

口味：甜中带咸，咸中带鲜

Stewed Duck in Earthen Pot

Ingredients:

1 duck (1200 g or 2.6 lb) with the insides removed
25 grams (4/5 oz) winter bamboo shoots
10 pieces of tender green vegetables
50 grams (3 1/2 tbsp) cooking oil
150 grams (8 tbsp) soy sauce
50 grams (3 1/3 tbsp) cooking wine
20 grams (1 3/4 tbsp) sugar
10 grams (2 tsp) sesame oil
50 grams (0.11 lb) sectioned scallions
10 grams (1/3 oz) sliced ginger
1000 grams (2 cups) water

Directions:

1. Remove the webs and tail of the duck. Tuck the duck's head tightly between its wings. Boil until bloody foam comes out. Take out and wash clean. Place the duck with the belly down in an earthen pot and put 10 g (1/5 of the total amount) of the scallions and all the ginger and bamboo shoots in the pot next to the duck.

2. Put the water in a pot and heat over strong fire. Add the soy sauce, sugar, cooking wine and bring to a boil. Skim off the foam. Pour the soup into the earthen pot already placed with the duck, put on the lid of the earthen pot to heat over strong fire. When it boils, turn to a low fire and simmer for 3 hours or until the meat becomes really soft.

3. Pick out the scallions and ginger and turn over the duck so that the belly side is up. Pick out the bamboo shoots and cut into slices to place on the belly. Quick-boil the tender vegetables and place them on the duck belly.

4. Put the oil in a wok and heat. Add the remaining scallions and stir-fry until the scallions turn yellow. Sprinkle the oil on the duck and leave out the scallions. Now sprinkle on the sesame oil as well.

Features: The duck maintains its shape while the meat has totally come loose from the bones. Rich but not greasy.
Taste: With a slight sweet touch in an otherwise salty dish. Simply delicious.

姆油鸭
Stewed Duck in Earthen Pot

三鲜鸭条

主料：净膛鸭1只（约1000克）

辅料：青椒75克、胡萝卜75克、火腿50克

调料：油100克、盐4克、味精1克、清汤150克、湿淀粉10克、料酒10克

制作：①锅内放入冷水置旺火上，放入鸭煮熟后捞出，去头、颈、爪。冷却后从背部剖开，剔去所有的骨头，切成1厘米宽、4厘米长的条。青椒切成1厘米宽的条。胡萝卜和火腿切成1厘米见方、5厘米长的条备用。

②锅置旺火上烧热放入75克油，待油温升至七成热时放入鸭条略炒，放入料酒、盐、清汤及青椒、笋、火腿，加盖焖约5分钟。掀盖收汁，待汤汁粘稠后用湿淀粉勾芡，淋上少许麻油，翻炒几下出锅装盘即成。

特点：色彩鲜艳，鸭条肥嫩

口味：咸鲜适口

Braised Duck Slices

Ingredients:

1 duck (1000 g or 2.2 lb), with the inside removed
75 grams (0.165 lb) green peppers
75 grams (0.165 lb) carrots
50 grams (0.11 lb) ham
100 grams (7 tbsp) cooking oil
4 grams (2/3 tsp) salt
1 gram (1/4 tsp) MSG
150 grams (10 tbsp) water
10 grams (2 tsp) mixture of cornstarch and water
10 grams (2 tsp) cooking wine

Directions:

1. Put cold water in a pot over a strong fire. Place the duck in the pot and boil until it is done. Remove the head, neck and webs. Cut open from the back and remove all the bones. Cut duck into shreds 4 cm (1.6 inches) long and 1 cm (0.4 inch) wide. Cut the green peppers into shreds also 1 cm (0.4 inch) wide. Cut the carrots and ham into shreds 5 cm (2 inches) long and 1 cm (0.4 inch) thick and wide.

2. Heat 75 g (5 1/2 tbsp) of oil to 180-200℃ (355-390°F) and stir-fry the duck shreds. Add the cooking wine, salt, water, green peppers, carrots and ham, and cover the lid to cook for 5 minutes. Take off the wok lid to reduce the liquid. When the liquid becomes thick, add the mixture of cornstarch and water. Sprinkle on a few drops of sesame oil and turn over several times. Now serve.

Features: Beautifully colored. The duck is rich and tender.
Taste: Salty and delicious.

三鲜鸭条
Braised Duck Slices

碧螺春炖鸭

主料：净膛鸭半只（约 600 克）

辅料：碧螺春茶叶（用其它绿茶也可）30 克

调料：盐 5 克、味精 2 克、清汤 1000 克

制作：①用沸水 500 克将茶叶泡开。

②将鸭斩成 4 厘米见方的块，入开水锅中煮出血沫，捞出后用清水冲洗干净。

③取砂锅一只，倒入碧螺春茶叶和水，放入鸭块，加盐、味精、清汤加盖上旺火烧开后转小火炖 2-3 小时，以锅内汤不沸但有小气泡上浮为宜。

特点：清香扑鼻，肥而不腻，酥烂脱骨

口味：咸鲜适口

Braised Duck with Green Tea

Ingredients:

1/2 duck (about 600 g or 1.3 lb), inside removed
30 grams (1 oz) green tea
5 grams (5/6 tsp) salt
2 grams (1/2 tsp) MSG
1000 grams (2 cups) water

Directions:

1. Stew the tea with 500 g (1 cup) of boiling water.

2. Cut the duck into square chunks 4 cm (1.6 inches) wide on each side and boil in a pot until blood foam comes out. Take out and wash clean.

3. Place the tea leaves and tea water in an earthen pot, and add the duck chunks, salt, MSG and water. Put on the cover and bring to a boil. Turn to a low fire to simmer for 2-3 hours. Best to keep the liquid at a heat where small air bubbles rise instead of boiling.

Features: Strongly aromatic and refreshing. Rich but not greasy, the meat is really soft.

Taste: Salty and delicious.

碧螺春炖鸭
Braised Duck with Green Tea

金银鸭片

主料：净膛鸭 1 只

辅料：火腿 200 克

调料：料酒 10 克、盐 2 克、味精 1 克、湿淀粉 15 克、麻油 10 克、葱 10 克、姜 15 克、清汤 100 克

制作：①锅内放入冷水置旺火上，放入鸭煮出血水，捞出洗净。将锅中水掉倒，重新加水，将鸭煮熟捞出晾凉，带皮切下鸭胸脯肉。

②将葱切段，姜切片。火腿切成 6 厘米长、1.5 厘米宽、0.2 厘米厚的片。将鸭脯切成 6 厘米长、0.3 厘米厚的片。

③鸭脯片和火腿片片片相间地排列成拱形码入碗中，加入料酒、盐、味精、清汤、葱段、姜片，上笼蒸 30 分钟取出。

④拣去葱、姜，滗出汤汁，翻扣在盘中。锅置旺火上倒入汤汁，烧开后用湿淀粉勾成薄芡，淋上麻油，浇在鸭上即成。

特点：红白相间，鲜香可口

口味：咸鲜适口

Duck Slices with Ham

Ingredients：

1 duck (1000 g or 2.4 lb) with the insides removed
200 grams (0.44 lb) ham
10 grams (2 tsp) cooking wine
2 grams (1/3 tsp) salt
1 gram (1/4 tsp) MSG
15 grams (1 tbsp) mixture of cornstarch and water
10 grams (2 tsp) sesame oil
10 grams (1/3 oz) sectioned scallions
15 grams (1/2 oz) sliced ginger
100 grams (6 tbsp) water

Directions：

1. Put cold water in a pot over a strong fire. Place the duck in the pot and boil until bloody foam comes out. Take out and wash clean. Get rid of the water in the pot and refill with fresh water. Boil the duck until it is done. Take out and let dry. Cut the breast meat off. (The rest of the duck can be used to make soup if so desired.)

2. Cut the ham into slices 6 cm (2.4 inches) long, 1.5 cm (0.6 inch) wide and 0.2 cm (0.08 inch) thick. Cut the breast into slices 6 cm (2.4 inches) long and 0.3 cm (0.12 inch) thick.

3. Place each duck breast slice between every two slices of ham in a bowl, add the cooking wine, salt, MSG, water, scallions and ginger, and steam for 30 minutes.

4. Pick out the scallions and ginger, carefully pour out the liquid and put the duck and ham on a plate by turning the bowl upside down. Heat the liquid to a boil, thicken it with the mixture of cornstarch and water, add the sesame oil and sprinkle it on the duck and ham.

Features：Nice combination of red and white colors and delicious.

Taste：Salty to the right taste.

咸水鹅

主料：净膛鹅 1 只（约 1000 克左右）

调料：盐 200 克、葱段 10 克、姜块 15 克、花椒 5 克、味精 5 克

制作：①将鹅放入盆内用 100 克盐在鹅腹内、外皮擦抹均匀，腌渍 24 小时取出，放入开水锅中煮出血沫捞出，洗净。

②锅内放入清水、盐、葱段、姜块（拍松）、花椒和鹅一起烧开后撇去浮沫，加盖转小火焖约 45 分钟，熄火后再焖约 1 小时捞出。

③将鹅切成四块，放在大汤碗中，取原汤及开水按 1:2 比例对成新汤加入味精，倒入汤碗中浸没鹅体，晾凉。

④食用时取出，斩成 5 厘米长、1 厘米宽的块装盘即成。

特点：肥而不腻，肉质鲜嫩

口味：以咸为主

Salted Goose

Ingredients:

1 goose (about 1000 g or 2.4 lb) with the insides removed
200 grams (0.44 lb) salt
10 grams (1/3 oz) sectioned scallions
15 grams (1/2 oz) ginger chunks
5 grams (1/6 oz) Chinese prickly ash
5 grams (1 1/4 tsp) MSG

Directions:

1. Put the goose in a basin. Use 100 g (0.22 lb) of the salt to rub its inside and outside and then marinate for 24 hours. Boil it until bloody foam comes out. Take out and wash clean.

2. Put fresh water in the pot, add the remaining salt, scallions, ginger (crushed to soften it), and Chinese prickly ash along with the goose and bring to boil. Skim off the foam, put on the cover and simmer over a low fire for 45 minutes. Turn off the fire but leave the pot covered for 1 hour. Take out the goose.

3. Cut the goose into 4 portions and place in a soup bowl. Use the original liquid and add boiling water at the ratio of 1 to 2 to make a soup. Add the MSG and pour into the soup bowl with the goose in it to submerge the goose. Let it cool off.

4. When serving, take the goose out of the soup, cut into chunks 5 cm (2 inches) long and 1 cm (0.4 inch) wide.

Features: Rich but not greasy. The meat is really tender.
Taste: Salty.

咸水鹅
Salted Goose

鸡蛋羹

主料：鸡蛋 5 只（约 300 克）

辅料：清汤 500 克

调料：盐 3 克、味精 2 克、葱末 5 克、麻油 5 克

制作：①取大汤碗一只，将鸡蛋磕入碗内并打散加盐、味精、清汤再打均匀。

②将汤碗置笼屉内用大汽蒸约 15 分钟后取出撒上葱末，淋上麻油即成。

特点：色淡黄，鸡蛋鲜嫩，入口即化

口味：咸鲜适口

Steamed Egg Soup

Ingredients：

5 eggs

500 grams (1 cup) water

3 grams (1/2 tsp) salt

2 grams (1/2 tsp) MSG

5 grams (1/6 oz) finely cut scallions

5 grams (1 tsp) sesame oil

Directions：

1. Whip the eggs in a large bowl. Add the salt, MSG and water and mix well.

2. Place the bowl in a steamer and cook for 15 minutes. Take out, spread the scallions and sprinkle on the sesame oil and the dish is ready.

Features： Light yellow in color, the egg is very tender and melts away as soon as it goes into the mouth.

Taste： Salty and delicious.

鸡蛋羹
Steamed Egg Soup

水煮荷包蛋

主料：鸡蛋 10 只

调料：熟油 5 克、盐 2 克、味精 1 克、葱末 5 克

制作：①锅内放冷水置旺火上烧开，转小火，逐个磕入鸡蛋，并用手勺轻轻推动，以免粘锅，待鸡蛋浮起后加锅盖再焖 2 分钟将鸡蛋捞入汤碗内。

②将原汤用大火烧开，撇去浮沫，加入盐、味精、葱末、油，倒入汤碗内即成。

特点：色白汤清，鸡蛋外滑里嫩

口味：咸鲜适口

Poached Egg

Ingredients：

10 eggs

5 grams (1 tsp) previously cooked oil

2 grams (1/3 tsp) salt

1 gram (1/4 tsp) MSG

5 grams (1/6 oz) finely cut scallions

Directions：

1. Heat water over strong fire and turn to low fire when the water boils. One by one, crack the eggs into the boiling water and push them gently with a ladle so as not to let the eggs get stuck to the bottom of the pot. When they rise, put on the pot cover for 2 minutes. Drop the eggs into a soup bowl.

2. Heat the liquid to a boiling point, skim off the egg foam, add the salt, MSG, scallions and previously cooked oil. Pour liquid onto the eggs.

Features：White in color, the eggs are slippery outside and tender inside.

Taste：Salty to the right taste.

蛋卷

主料：鸡蛋 2 只

辅料：肉末 200 克

调料：油 10 克、盐 4 克、味精 1 克、葱姜末各 3 克、干淀粉 10 克

制作：①鸡蛋磕入碗中打散。炒锅置小火上烧热，抹上油，倒入蛋液迅速转动炒锅制成蛋皮。肉末内放盐、味精、葱姜末搅拌上劲。

②蛋皮平铺在砧板上撒上干淀粉，抹匀，铺上肉末抹平，卷成长卷装盘上笼蒸 8 分钟，取出斜切成菱形，装盘即可。

特点：香嫩

口味：咸鲜适口

Egg Rolls

Ingredients：

2 eggs

200 grams (0.44 lb) ground meat

10 grams (2 tsp) cooking oil

4 grams (2/3 tsp) salt

1 gram (1/4 tsp) MSG

3 grams (1/10 oz) finely cut scallions

3 grams (1/10 oz) chopped ginger

10 grams (1 1/2 tbsp) dry cornstarch

Directions：

1. Whip the eggs in a bowl. Heat the wok over low fire, add oil, pour in the whipped eggs and quickly rotate the wok to make the eggs coat the inside of the wok. The eggs will later be used as the wrapping. Add salt, MSG, scallions and ginger into the ground meat, and stir well until the mixture becomes sticky.

2. Put the egg wrapping flat on a chopping board, spread the dry cornstarch evenly on top of it, and then evenly spread on the ground meat. Roll meat up into a long roll. Place roll around the edge of a plate to make a ring and steam for 8 minutes. Take off and cut roll into diamond shapes to serve on a plate.

Features：Delicious and appetizing.

Taste：Salty to the right taste.

蛋卷
Egg Rolls

蛋饺

主料：鸡蛋 5 只

辅料：肉末 500 克

调料：盐 5 克、味精 2 克、姜葱末各 5 克、油 25 克

制作：①肉末加盐、味精、姜葱末搅拌上劲备用。

②鸡蛋磕入碗中加油打散，取直径 8 厘米的大汤勺置小火上烧热，倒入少量蛋液，转动汤勺使蛋液凝结成蛋皮，放入 25 克肉末，将蛋皮对折即成半圆形蛋饺。再烧 1 分钟，置于盘中。照以上方法依次做好其余的蛋饺，然后上笼蒸约 10 分钟即可食用。也可置于汤中烧开后食用。

特点：色淡黄，形如饺

口味：咸鲜适口

Egg Dumplings

Ingredients：

5 eggs

500 grams (1.1 lb) ground meat

5 grams (5/6 tsp) salt

2 grams (1/2 tsp) MSG

5 grams (1/6 oz) finely cut scallions

5 grams (1/6 oz) chopped ginger

25 grams (1 2/3 tbsp) cooking oil

Directions：

1. Add the salt, MSG, scallions and ginger to the meat and stir well until substance becomes sticky.

2. Whip the eggs in a bowl and mix with the oil as follows: Put some of the oil in a large steel soup ladle 8 cm (3.2 inches) in diameter and heat over low fire, then add into the ladle some of the whipped eggs. Turn the ladle frequently to allow the eggs to coat the sides of the ladle and thus form a small wrapping for the meat. Put in 25 g (5/6 oz) of the meat and fold the wrapping in the ladle with the help of a pair of chopsticks to make a dumpling. Heat one more minute and place on a plate. Repeat this procedure until all the whipped egg and ground meat are used. Steam for 10 minutes and the egg dumplings are ready to be served. Alternatively, they can be put in soup and when the soup boils, they are ready to be served.

Features：Light yellow in color and beautiful in shape.

Taste：Salty and delicious.

蛋饺
Egg Dumplings

五香茶叶蛋

主料：鸡蛋 10 只

调料：红茶茶叶 25 克、大料 3 只、桂皮 15 克、酱油 150 克、糖 100 克、盐 5 克、味精 3 克、葱段 10 克、姜块 15 克

制作：①锅内放入冷水置旺火上，放入鸡蛋，烧开后转小火焖 5 分钟捞出，放冷水中凉透。将鸡蛋置于砧板上用刀背轻轻将蛋壳拍碎裂。

②茶叶、大料、桂皮用纱布包好，放入锅内，加酱油、糖、味精、葱段、姜块（拍松）、鸡蛋，用大火烧开，5 分钟后转小火焖 30 分钟。

③将鸡蛋及汤一齐倒入盆中，食时捞出去壳即可。

特点：色泽暗红，鲜香可口

口味：咸甜适口

Five-flavored Egg with Tea

Ingredients：
10 eggs
25 grams (5/6 oz) red tea leaves
3 pieces of star anise
15 grams (1/2 oz) cassia bark
150 grams (11 tbsp) soy sauce
100 grams (0.22 lb) sugar
5 grams (5/6 tsp) salt
3 grams (3/4 tsp) MSG
10 grams (1/3 oz) sectioned scallions
15 grams (1/2 oz) crushed ginger chunks

Directions：
1. Heat cold water in a pot. Put the unpeeled eggs in and turn to a low fire after water boils to cook the eggs for 15 minutes. Take out the eggs and cool them off completely in cold water. Put the eggs on a chopping board and gently crack them with a big spoon or the back of the kitchen knife and then peel them.

2. Wrap the tea, star anise and cassia bark in a piece of gauze. Place this in the pot. Add the soy sauce, MSG, sugar, scallions, ginger and eggs and bring to a boil over a strong fire. Turn to a low fire 5 minutes later and then simmer over the low fire for 30 minutes.

3. Put both the eggs and the sauce in a basin and eat the eggs whenever one wishes.

Features： Dark red in color, the eggs are simply aromatic and refreshing.

Taste： Salty and delicious.

蛋松

主料：鸡蛋 5 只

调料：油 2000 克（实耗 100 克）、盐 2 克、味精 1 克

制作：①将鸡蛋磕入碗中，加盐、味精打散备用。

②炒锅置旺火上烧热，倒入油，待油温升至七成热时，一手持碗使蛋液成线状淋入油锅中，另一手持手勺不断搅动油，使蛋液成丝状，浮起变黄后捞出，控净油，然后再放在餐巾纸上，压干油后，用手拉松拉散即可。

特点：酥松香脆

口味：咸鲜适口

Fluffy Egg

Ingredients：
5 eggs
2000 grams (4 cups) oil (only 1/20 to be consumed)
2 grams (1/3 tsp) salt
1 gram (1/4 tsp) MSG

Directions：

1. Whip the eggs in a bowl, add the salt and MSG.

2. Heat the oil over strong fire to 180-200℃ (355-390°F) and carefully pour the whipped eggs into the oil to allow the egg paste to drip continuously until all of it is in the wok. While pouring with one hand, use the other to hold a ladle to keep stirring the egg paste in the oil so that the paste will take the form of a thread. When it rises in the oil and turns yellow, take it out and drain off the oil. Place the fluffy egg on a paper napkin, press out the oil, loosen it with your hand and it is ready to serve.

Features：Soft and crispy.
Taste：Salty and delicious.

虎皮蛋

主料：鸡蛋 12 只

调料：油 1000 克（实耗 75 克）、料酒 10 克、盐 1.5 克、酱油 15 克、味精 1 克、清汤 500 克、麻油 10 克、干淀粉 15 克、湿淀粉 30 克、葱段 5 克

制作：①锅内放入冷水置旺火上放入鸡蛋煮熟，捞出剥去壳，在汤中略浸后捞出，滚上干淀粉。

②锅置旺火上烧热，倒入油，待油温升至七成热时，放入鸡蛋炸至起泡呈虎皮色捞起。

③原锅留油 25 克，下葱段，加酱油、料酒、盐、味精、清汤放入鸡蛋烧透，用湿淀粉勾芡，淋上麻油，装盘即成。

特点：色如虎皮，清爽香嫩

口味：甜咸适口

Egg with Brown Sauce

Ingredients：

12 eggs

1000 grams (2 cups) cooking oil (only 5 1/2 tbsp or under 1/13 to be consumed)

10 grams (2 tsp) cooking oil

1 1/2 grams (1/4 tsp) salt

15 grams (1 3/4 tsp) soy sauce

1 gram (1/4 tsp) MSG

500 grams (1 cup) water

10 grams (2 tsp) sesame oil

15 grams (1 3/4 tbsp) dry cornstarch

30 grams (1 tbsp) mixture of cornstarch and water

5 grams (1/6 oz) sectioned scallions

Directions：

1. Boil the eggs until they are done. Remove the shells, soak in the boiled water and dust with dry cornstarch.

2. Heat the oil in a wok over strong fire to 180-200℃ (355-390°F) and deep-fry the unbroken eggs until they change to brown color with creases on them.

3. Keep 25 g (1 2/3 tbsp) of oil in the wok. Put in the scallions, add the soy sauce, cooking wine, salt, MSG, water and eggs and cook well. Thicken the sauce with the mixture of cornstarch and water. Sprinkle on the sesame oil and put on a plate to serve.

Features：The eggs have a color like tiger fur and taste very refreshing.

Taste：Salty to the right taste.

虎皮蛋
Egg with Brown Sauce

计量换算表

1磅	1盎司	1打兰	1格令
约454克	约28克	约1.8克	约0.06克

调料 ml 勺	水	油	酱油	醋	料酒	盐	味精	砂糖	淀粉
1ml勺	约1克	约0.9克	约1.2克	约1克	约1克	约1.2克	约0.7克	约0.9克	约0.4克
5ml勺	约5克	约4.5克	约6克	约5克	约5克	约6.3克	约3.7克	约4.5克	约2克
15ml勺	约15克	约13.5克	约18克	约15克	约15克	约18.5克	约11克	约13克	约6克
50ml勺	约50克	约55克	约60克	约50克	约50克	约63克		约42克	约20克
500ml勺	约500克	约549克	约600克	约500克	约500克	约630克			

A comparison of the weight systems

US system	1 grain(gr)	1ounce(oz)	1pound(lb)
Metric	0.065 gram(g)	28.35 grams(g)	454 grams(g)

A conversion table for measuring Chinese cooking ingredients*

ingredients cornstarch	water	ckg oil	soy sauce	vinegar	ckg wine	salt	MSG	sugar	cornstarch
1 pinch/1ml	1g	0.9g	1.2g	1g	1g	1.2g	0.7g	0.9g	0.4g
1tsp/5ml	5g	4.5g	6g	5g	5g	6.3g	3.7g	4.5g	2g
1tbsp/15ml	15g	13.5g	18g	15g	15g	18.5g	11g	13g	6g
1.76floz/50ml	50g	55g	60g	50g	50g	63g		42g	20g
3.52floz/1cup	500g	549g	600g	500g	500g	630g			

*All figures in grams given here are approximate as the exact equivalents will result
in too many digits after the decimal point.

在编辑《学做中国菜》系列丛书的过程中，得到了苏州饭店的大力支持和帮助。作为苏州市旅游业的骨干企业苏州饭店已有数十年的历史，饭店拥有一流的烹饪厨师，经验丰富，技艺精湛。今借此书出版之机，我们对苏州饭店给予的支持，深表感谢！

We wish to thank the Suzhou Hotel, which kindly provided strong support and assistance to the compilation of the *Learn to Cook Chinese Dishes* series. As a major tourist hotel in the city of Suzhou, the Suzhou Hotel has a history of dozens of years and is serviced by experienced first-class chefs.

图书在版编目(CIP)数据

学做中国菜·禽蛋类/《学做中国菜》编委会编.-北京：外文出版社,1999
ISBN 7-119-02492-2

Ⅰ.学… Ⅱ.学… Ⅲ.禽蛋-烹饪-中国-汉、英对照 Ⅳ.TS972.1
中国版本图书馆 CIP 数据核字(1999)第 48188 号

Members of the Editorial Board:
Sun Jiaping Lu Qinpu
Sun Shuming Liu Chun'gen
Lan Peijin
Dish preparation and text:
Zhu Deming Wen Jinshu
Zhu Guifu Zhang Guomin
Zhang Guoxiang Xu Rongming
Cao Gang
Editor: Sun Shuming
English translation and editing:
Huang Youyi Foster Stockwell Cong Guoling
Design: Sun Shuming
Photography: Sun Shuming Liu Chun'gen Lan Peijin
Cover design: Wang Zhi

编委：孙建平 鲁钦甫 孙树明
　　　刘春根 兰佩瑾
菜肴制作及撰文：朱德明 温金树
　　　　　　　朱桂福 张国民
　　　　　　　张国祥 徐荣明
　　　　　　　曹　刚
责任编辑：孙树明
英文翻译：黄友义 卓柯达 丛国玲
设计：孙树明
摄影：孙树明 刘春根 兰佩瑾
封面设计：王　志

First Edition 2000

Learn to Cook Chinese Dishes
—Poultry & Eggs

ISBN 7-119-02492-2

©Foreign Languages Press
Published by Foreign Languages Press
24 Baiwanzhuang Road, Beijing 100037, China
Home Page：http://www.flp.com.cn
E-mail Addresses：info @ flp.com.cn
　　　　　　　　sales @ flp.com.cn
Printed in the People's Republic of China

学做中国菜·禽蛋类
《学做中国菜》编委会 编
© 外文出版社
外文出版社出版
(中国北京百万庄大街 24 号)邮政编码 100037
外文出版社网页：http://www.flp.com.cn
外文出版社电子邮件地址：info @ flp.com.cn
　　　　　　　　　　　　sales @ flp.com.cn
北京骏马行图文中心制版
天时印刷(深圳)有限公司印制
2000 年 (24 开)第一版
2000 年第一版第一次印刷
(英汉)
ISBN 7-119-02492-2/J·1516 (外)
08000 (精)